ᴛʜᴇQuotable
STONER

THE Quotable
STONER

MORE THAN **1,100** BAKED, LIT-UP, and ZONKED-OUT QUOTES IN TRIBUTE to

(AND AS A RESULT OF) SMOKING WEED

HOLDEN BLUNTS

Aadamsmedia
Avon, Massachusetts

Published by
Adams Media, a division of F+W Media, Inc.
57 Littlefield Street, Avon, MA 02322. U.S.A.
www.adamsmedia.com

ISBN 10: 1-4405-2589-7
ISBN 13: 978-1-4405-2589-6
eISBN 10: 1-4405-2732-6
eISBN 13: 978-1-4405-2732-6

Printed in the United States of America.

10 9 8 7 6 5 4 3 2 1

Library of Congress Cataloging-in-Publication Data

Blunts, Holden.
The quotable stoner / Holden Blunts.
p. cm.
ISBN 978-1-4405-2589-6
1. Marijuana—Humor. 2. Marijuana—Quotations. I. Title.
PN6231.M24B58 2011
818'.602—dc22
2011010386

All interior illustrations © Jupiterimages Corporation

This book is available at quantity discounts for bulk purchases.
For information, please call 1-800-289-0963.

DEDICATION

For Sunshine and her bagels,

For Jenny Lee and her song,

For pot.

CONTENTS

INTRODUCTION

As stoners, we live quite the life. We have the power to dictate how our day goes—a terrible day turns into no big deal when we toke up. Everything is instantly better. Nonsmokers sure as hell can't say that.

And sure, we're not the best at remembering things . . . picking up our brother from soccer practice, where we left the remote, what day of the week it is, how long that sandwich has been sitting in the fridge. But one thing's for sure: We come up with some hilarious shit when we're high.

The quotes in this book will make you feel at home in your basement. Or in the supply room at work. Or your buddy's garage. Really anywhere you inhale the almighty leaf. And your buddies may not be famous, but you'll feel like they're right by your side when you read all about pot straight from the mouths of presidents, politicians, celebrities, and other stoners from around the world.

Take a look-see at this ubiquitous quote from a founding father:

"Make the most of the Indian hemp seed and sow it everywhere."
—George Washington

Yeah, it probably came from a letter that reads: "I am very glad to hear that the Gardener has saved so much of the St. foin seed, and that of the India Hemp. Make the most you can of both. . . . The Hemp may be sown any where," but still. Our first president loved pot. And I'm sticking to it.

So pack a bowl, spread the love, and inhale some wisdom from other ganja lovers who have been there and done that . . . over and over and over and over again.

CHAPTER 1

POT CULTURE

"I don't know what they have done to pot in the last thirty years, but it rocks!"

—Meryl Streep as Jane, *It's Complicated*

The average narc might think there isn't much "culture" to pot, but we know what's up. Anyone who's ever burned through a Tuesday smoking an eighth of Egyptian Christmas Tree and watching sixteen straight hours of cable courtesy of the downstairs neighbor knows that America is built on weed. Just look at some of the potheads who have made their mark on the lives we live—Clinton. Clapton. Spicoli. Hey, the dude with the Jew-fro from *Pineapple Express* has built an entire career on pot culture—without selling so much as a dime bag. From the poorhouse to the White House, everyone smokes weed, man—and some of these people have had some pretty interesting shit to say.

So roll yourself a fat one, grab yourself a Dr Pepper and some of those Taco Bell–flavored Doritos, and treat yourself to some witty ramblings from and about some of our favorite pot heads in popular culture.

"This is not '60s marijuana anymore. We're finding marijuana with a THC content in the 20s—20 percentile. We're talking back in the '60s and '70s of 3–4 percent THC. Now it's in the 20s. This is very potent stuff now."

—MARK R. TROUVILLE, MIAMI DEA SPECIAL AGENT IN CHARGE

FINE FUMES: ACAPULCO GOLD

This classic strain *is* your grandfather's sativa. The awesomely ill spread of sativa strains we have today most likely wouldn't be possible had it not been for this forerunner. As the name suggests, it's a Mexican national that we are stoked got across the border.

"That stoner thing cuts across political lines."

—CHEECH MARIN

"The best thing it does is just makes you open to the human experience."

—KEVIN SMITH, *SMODCAST*

"Experience is only half of experience."

—JOHANN WOLFGANG VON GOETHE

"I got this at the bake sale for the environment that those boys were having. You know you don't often see white boys with the dreadlocks."

—JULIE WHITE AS JUDY WITWICKY IN *TRANSFORMERS 2: REVENGE OF THE FALLEN*

"The person who doesn't scatter the morning dew will not comb gray hairs."

—PROVERB, OFTEN ATTRIBUTED TO HUNTER S. THOMPSON

"They have done study after study after study on this issue of marijuana—every administration since, like, FDR. You know what they found out? It makes you want to eat SpaghettiOs right out of the saucepan. That's the worst thing."

—BILL MAHER

"I'm really good at chillin'. I noticed that I can sit for hours. I'm really good at that. I think in life that there's too much pressure to produce and have something to show for yourself. I would definitely put myself in a situation where I didn't have to have a lot of productivity."

—MITCH HEDBERG, SAUSAGE FACTORY: THE COLLEGE CRIER'S INFAMOUS INTERVIEWS OF THE FREAKS AND THE FAMOUS

"You can stump any stoner with one question on any show: 'Alright, stoners, you ready for the big money question: What were we just talking about?'"

—JIM BREUER

"Life seems to be very complicated in every place of the world. Most of us are anxious from time to time. Most of us are depressed from time to time. We want to change that. In many cases, such a change can be brought forward by cannabis. That's why people use it."

—RAPHAEL MECHOULAM, PIONEERING THC RESEARCHER

"My number one rule for living is have fun at all times."

—SNOOP DOGG

"Can we admit that medical marijuana is a complete fucking joke? . . . The clinics don't even try anymore. They'll try to feign a healthy environment, like, they'll have a green cross, but then right next to it in, like, old school Beastie Boys graffiti font it'll be like 'Get your fucking smoke on, dawg!'"

—MOSHE KASHER, COMEDIAN

"Young people have finely tuned bullshit detectors, and nothing annoys young people more than adult hypocrisy, and on the issue of pot, adults, teachers, DARE educators, and politicians positively reek of it."

—DAN SAVAGE, *SKIPPING TOWARDS GOMORRAH*

"Like the vast majority of Americans, I have goals, aspirations, and desires that preclude spending all my time in bed, stoned out of my mind, watching *Showgirls* with Richard Lowry."

—DAN SAVAGE, *SKIPPING TOWARDS GOMORRAH*

"Life is lived indoors."

—KEVIN SMITH, *SMODCAST*

POT SPOTS: HOTBOX

Here's a really fun place you can make practically anywhere. And of course, since it's really fun, it's kinda dangerous. In a closed space, like a car or a bathroom, start smoking up with your buds. Let the smoke fill your hotbox and pretty soon you won't need to puff or pass. Just breathe. Fuck yeah. But yeah, it's also dangerous with the lack of breathable air thing.

"It gives you a whole new way of looking at the day."

—PETER FONDA AS WYATT, *EASY RIDER*

"For years and years, Arj Barker was high on life, but after a while I built up a tolerance. It just wasn't cutting the mustard any more."

—ARJ BARKER

"The older you do get, the more rules they going to try to get you to follow. You just gotta keep livin' man. L.I.V.I.N."

—MATTHEW MCCONAUGHEY AS WOODERSON, *DAZED AND CONFUSED*

"Mom, I'm selling weed. It's as close to recession-proof as it gets."

—HUNTER PARRISH AS SILAS, *WEEDS*

"That's the beauty of college these days, Tommy. You can major in Game Boy if you know how to bullshit."

—JEREMY PIVEN
AS DROZ IN *PCU*

"I know you don't smoke weed. I know this. But I'm going to get you high today 'cause it's Friday. You ain't got no job, and you ain't got shit to do."

—CHRIS TUCKER
AS SMOKEY, *FRIDAY*

"I love my FedEx guy 'cause he's a drug dealer and he don't even know it . . . and he's always on time."

—MITCH HEDBERG

"They say that the true pothead stops getting the munchies after a certain point. I mean the true pothead wouldn't even say the word 'munchies.' I don't know what the true pothead would say. 'Munchos' or 'hungries' or something. At any rate, I still love to eat when I'm high. So fuck you if you're too cool to get hungry when you're stoned."

—ANNA FARIS AS JANE,
SMILEY FACE

"If we are all gonna die anyway, shouldn't we be enjoying ourselves now? You know, I'd like to quit thinking of the present, like right now, as some minor insignificant preamble to something else."

—MARISSA RIBISI AS CYNTHIA
IN *DAZED AND CONFUSED*

FINE FUMES: BURNT POPCORN

College students are notoriously bad at cooking popcorn. In dormitories, it's floor after floor of terrible popcorn makers. You'd think they'd learn—it *is* a school. If you find yourself smelling this frequently in vertical living spaces, follow the scent toward some new friends. And then tell them to be more creative. Everyone knows what they're doing.

"I figure if I study high, take the test high, get high scores! Right?"

—REDMAN AS JAMAL
IN *HOW HIGH*

"In college . . . we would ride the buzz of endorphins, beer, and pot, acting giddy as we talked about Ultimate, barely able to contain our excitement."

—DAVID GESSNER, *SICK OF
NATURE*

"Link and I are cruising the mountain, bro, and figured we'd wheeze a little juice."

—PAULY SHORE AS STONEY,
ENCINO MAN

Kumar (Kal Penn): Meet the smokeless bong.

Harold (John Cho): You made this?

Kumar: You know I did. When you were slaving away at work, I was actually being a productive member of society.

—*HAROLD AND KUMAR ESCAPE
FROM GUANTANAMO BAY*

"There's only one 'return,' okay, and it ain't of the king. It's of the Jedi."

—JEFF ANDERSON AS RANDAL,
CLERKS II

"People keep looking at this as if it's just a bunch of potheads sitting around in the corner somewhere."

—MONTEL WILLIAMS

POT SPOTS: THE BERKSHIRES

Stoners take to mountains like mountain goats. Tucked away in the mountains of western Massachusetts, far from Boston and its accent, are a number of artistic communities that are very weed friendly. If you ever wondered why Karen Allen from Indiana Jones isn't acting anymore, it's because she's there, in Great Barrington, selling her knitwear.

"The only thing you have ever cared about in your life was nugs, chillin' and grindage."

—SEAN ASTIN AS DAVE,
ENCINO MAN

"It's, like, the rarest. It's almost a shame to smoke it. It's like killing a unicorn . . . with, like, a bomb."

—JAMES FRANCO AS SAUL,
PINEAPPLE EXPRESS

Sue (Paige Howard): What are you majoring in?

Joel (Martin Starr): Russian literature and Slavic languages.

Sue: Wow, that's really interesting. What career track is that?

Joel: Cabbie, hot dog vendor, marijuana delivery guy. The world is my oyster.

—ADVENTURELAND

"When pop culture began to embrace marijuana, to treat it either in a humorous fashion or kinda an ordinary fashion . . . you knew we were making progress because popular culture mimics, to some extent, changes that are already going on."

—KEITH STROUP,
NORML FOUNDER

"Forty million Americans smoke marijuana and the only ones who didn't like it were Judge Ginsburg, Clarence Thomas, and Bill Clinton."

—JAY LENO

"This will be the second time in my life that I'm going to don a blindfold, be shoved into a van, and arrive at a grow-op. Hey Mom, told you I didn't need college."

—KEVIN PEREIRA, ATTACK OF
THE SHOW!

"For centuries, marijuana has been used as a self-prescribed remedy for the terminal disease known as 'being alive.'"

—STEVE CARELL, THE DAILY SHOW WITH JON STEWART

"I have to be honest; I have contempt for pretty much every drug other than pot. I find drunk people gross. Most people with more than one drink in them aren't giggly, goofy, and happy the way people are with a puff of pot smoke in them. . . . At a party, I have so much fun stoned, flitting about—but once I sniff that first wave of drunkenness on someone, I'm out of there."

—SARAH SILVERMAN, THE BED-WETTER: STORIES OF COURAGE, REDEMPTION, AND PEE

Sookie (Claire Danes): "Dimebag." . . . Well that got your attention.

Igby (Kieran Culkin): Pavlov's pothead. . . . I hear the sound of a bong clink and my eyes begin to water.

—IGBY GOES DOWN

"I enjoy the way you can kind of transform into different identities with pot . . . sometimes when you're stuck in the same mode, getting high induces change."

—SHANNON HOON OF BLIND MELON

"CBGB is a state of mind."

—PATTI SMITH

"If you come to me and ask me, I'm going to tell you the truth because I have had tea. Lots of tea. Indian tea . . . and biscuits."

—ERIC IDLE AS DIRK MCQUICKLY (OF THE RUTLES) IN ALL YOU NEED IS CASH

"It was a high waking up in the morning and thinking, am I going to get arrested today, or am I going to make $4 million?"

—RICHARD STRATTON, EDITOR IN CHIEF, HIGH TIMES

"I'm a reefer refugee."

—EAGLE BILL, CHEROKEE MARIJUANA MEDICINE MAN

"In the past we have had a little smoke, the odd toke. . . . Everyone has a little smoke once in a while, you know. It's one of life's little pleasures."

—RHYS IFANS

"There's nothing even remotely naughty about it. It's like Sudafed. I was never interested in it. I just feel, honestly, people make a really big deal about it."

—MARY-LOUISE PARKER

"As much as drugs can do bad things, they can also bring people together."

—DENNIS HOPPER

"I went up to people who I thought might be Asian so I could hang out, but it turns out they were just stoned."

—MARGARET CHO

POT SPOTS: HAAD RIN
Cho said that during her Bonnaroo stand-up set, but there's another festival with a greater Asian audience makeup, and that's the monthly full-moon beach party at Haad Rin in Thailand. The weed, while not legal, isn't terribly frowned upon. The full moon has been freaking stoners out for thousands of years, and at Haad Rin, it's even trippier because you know everyone else is feeling it too.

"People think 'Puff the Magic Dragon' is about marijuana, and I know it's not because I co-wrote it."

—PETER YARROW

"It's surely not about drugs. I can tell you that at Cornell in 1959, no one smoked grass. I find the fact that people interpret it as a drug song annoying. It would be insidious to propagandize about drugs in a song for little kids."

—LEONARD LIPTON

"'Puff' is a reassertion of the sensibility that we shared in the Sixties, when people were caring and vulnerable and open."

—PETER YARROW

POT SPOTS: HANALEI, HI

Maybe we believe that "Puff the Magic Dragon" isn't about weed, but you can't deny that "Honalee" looks a lot like Hanalei, a city on the Hawaiian island of Kauai, which is said to have been a huge producer of marijuana up through the 1980s.

Jack Byrnes (Robert De Niro): Puff is just the name of the boy's magical dragon. . . . You a pothead, Focker?

Greg Focker (Ben Stiller): No, I pass on grass always. Well, not always.

—*MEET THE PARENTS*

"Go ahead and sleep on the power couch. Your training begins tomorrow, at the crack of noon."

—KYLE GASS AS KG IN *TENACIOUS D IN THE PICK OF DESTINY*

"People have one great blessing—obscurity—and not really too many people are thankful for it. Everybody is always taught to be thankful for their food and clothes and things like that, but not to be thankful for their obscurity."

—BOB DYLAN

Jay (Jason Mewes): Shit, bitch, we're gonna bust up that stage like a high school kegger. We're just gonna outwit La Fours, X-Men style.

   Brodie (Jason Lee): Should I call you "Logan," Weapon-X?

   Jay: No, "Wolverine"! Snikty snikty!

—*MALLRATS*

"There are no mistakes, only happy accidents."

—BOB ROSS

"If you got a problem with Willie Nelson, you got a problem with me."

—SNOOP DOGG

"I understand what Snoop's saying. It makes a lot of sense, and it's funny."

—WILLIE NELSON

Chapter 2

POT ETIQUETTE

"For the younger people here, it should be a treat. Make it a treat. If it's an everyday thing and it's easy to get, it takes the fun out of it."

—Sarah Silverman

The Boy Scouts' motto is "Be prepared." That's . . . that's good—it's just not really specific to them. It's more of a good first step for everything, ever. Maybe they should have gone with, "Boys can wear sashes too!"

They're right though: A little preparation is a good thing. Even the most antisocial stoners can benefit from some preparedness and knowing how to act appropriately with and around their weed. Even if you're growing your own, you're going to have to interact with someone to get some hardware—and not leave a trail.

We're lucky; our pot-loving culture is generally relaxed and accepting of newbie blunders, but there are some definite tips you can take to make sure you bake without getting beaten.

"We go through this every time I come here. I don't care what it's called. I just want a bag of fuckin' weed."

—ALLEN COVERT AS ALEX IN
GRANDMA'S BOY

"You have to allot at least seven and three-quarters minutes of fake interest in the person holding the weed. Say something nice about them or their stuff, like, 'Cool pipe,' or, 'Wow, that's a neat lizard.'"

—DOUG BENSON, ARJ BARKER,
AND TONY CAMIN, THE
MARIJUANA-LOGUES: EVERY-
THING ABOUT POT THAT WE
COULD REMEMBER

"What you're about to receive is called a 'blowback.' I'm going to blow the smoke into your mouth and you're going to inhale very deeply. And hold the smoke in your lungs and you will . . . not . . . cough. . . . Understood?"

—ALICE EVE AS ALICE IN
STARTER FOR 10

"I just tell the people who do it not to do it when you have a lot of important things to do. That should be your playtime. It's a luxury."

—AFROMAN

"Never take ecstasy, beer, Bacardi, weed, Pepto Bismol, Vivarin, Tums, Tagamet HB, Xanax, and Valium in the same day. It makes it difficult to sleep at night."

—EMINEM

"I learned to roll a joint in Europe, and I think I roll a joint pretty good . . . for a girl."

—HOLLY "G" OF
MARIJUANA RADIO

"It never occurred to you to put it in a Ziploc bag and sink it to the bottom of a shampoo bottle in your checked luggage, like we all do? Really?"

—AMY POEHLER ON *SATURDAY NIGHT LIVE*

"He held up a small pipe with a wide flattened bowl, and handed it to Gimli. 'Does that settle the score between us?' he said.

'Settle it!' cried Gimli. 'Most noble hobbit, it leaves me deep in your debt.'"

—J. R. R. TOLKIEN, *THE TWO TOWERS* (PIPPIN PACKS A BOWL.)

"Justice Is the Whim of the Judge is an axiom that I picked up a long time ago at the Columbia Law School in New York, where I also learned how to handle large sums of money and how to smoke marijuana in polite company without making a scene and acting like a junkie."

—HUNTER S. THOMPSON, *KINGDOM OF FEAR*

"I hefted its weight and smelled it, not really certain what the proper procedure might be. I looked like some backwoods hillbilly struggling to approve of a bottle of fine French Bordeaux."

—DUSTIN DIAMOND, *BEHIND THE BELL*

FINE FUMES: SKUNK #1

Smelling way better than you'd expect from this original gangsta, skunk is a 3:1 sativa-indica hybrid. In the UK, "skunk" is overused by officials and media to describe any really powerful hybrid—apparently there's a lot of dank getting imported over there. I'm thinking of getting imported too.

"Puff puff, give. Puff puff, give. You fuckin' up the rotation."

—CHRIS TUCKER AS SMOKEY,
FRIDAY

Kenny Davis (Harland Williams): Hey, if I'm not back in ten minutes, call the police.

Thurgood Jenkins (Dave Chappelle): If he's not back in ten minutes, we're calling Domino's!

—HALF BAKED

"There are obvious times when you don't want people getting high. I wouldn't want my surgeon getting high before he operated on me. That's an example of when it's bad."

—DAVID CROSS

"A black man would never dream of talking to the police, high. That's a waste of weed."

—DAVE CHAPPELLE

HIGH CREDENTIALS: DAVE CHAPPELLE

Chappelle is loved for his stoner-friendly sketch show—which was positively tits, but we can't forget his big break: the stoner favorite, *Robin Hood: Men in Tights*, when he was just twenty years old. Proving he's always been good at impressions, we see both his Malcolm X and his Bruce Lee as he travels around Sherwood Forest. You should feel a little high just thinking about that.

"Treat the wife, treat somebody else's wife. It's a lot more fun if you don't get caught."

—JASON STATHAM AS BACON IN
LOCK, STOCK AND TWO SMOKING
BARRELS

"The burgers wouldn't taste as good if you weren't there."

—KAL PENN AS KUMAR IN HAR-
OLD AND KUMAR GO TO WHITE
CASTLE

"People tell me that I look like a cop, alright? They say that I have cop face. There's nothing I can do about it. But you just look like a gay guy, so it'll go much smoother that way."

—MICHAEL SHOWALTER,
MICHAEL AND MICHAEL HAVE
ISSUES

Man Stoner (Tommy Chong): You wanna get high, man?

Pedro (Cheech Marin): Does Howdy Doody got wooden balls, man?

—UP IN SMOKE

Victor "Vic" Vance (Dorian Missick): The reefer is under my bed.

Jerry Martinez (Felix Solis): Oh, genius! Great hiding place! What are you, fifteen?

—GRAND THEFT AUTO:
VICE CITY STORIES

"If you ever go to a hotel, be sure to bring your own towel."

—VERNON CHATMAN AS TOW-
ELIE, SOUTH PARK

"They'd wedged towels beneath the door—their usual modus operandi—but the scent of pot had somehow penetrated and wafted into a security guard's nostrils."

—GRACE SLICK, ROCK SINGER,
SOMEBODY TO LOVE

"Hogging the reefer to yourself is often known as 'Bogarting,' punishable by death."

—SETH MAXWELL MALICE,
DAZED AND CONFUSED (BOOK)

"Hey! Don't bogart that Squishee!"

—PAMELA HAYDEN AS MIL-
HOUSE ON THE SIMPSONS

"Never pass a microscopic roach."

—SETH MAXWELL MALICE,
DAZED AND CONFUSED (BOOK)

"I think pot should be legalized, but I think the promotion of party culture is irresponsible."

—KRIST NOVOSELIC OF NIRVANA

"You sound like a man with a vision. Care to pass that bong over this way?"

—PAUL VIXIE, AUTHOR AND
SOFTWARE ARCHITECT

"You should never throw a bong, kid. Ever."

—PETER DANTE AS DANTE IN
GRANDMA'S BOY

"I always smoke pot with you, all of you, *my* pot, all the time. So why shouldn't I make some money offa you? I'm providing you schmucks with such a crucial service. Plus I'm developing valuable entrepreneurial skills for my *future*. *Plus* I'm like providing you with precious memories of youth, for when you're fucking *old*."

—DENNIS, IN KENNETH LONER-
GAN'S THIS IS OUR YOUTH

"First of all, you can calm down a little. Relax. Create the illusion that we're friends talking."

—JORGE GARCIA AS A DRUG
DEALER ON CURB YOUR
ENTHUSIASM

"Dumb slut, that was half a jay of good moody you just wasted!"

—STEVEN WEBBER AS JACK IN
REEFER MADNESS: THE MOVIE
MUSICAL

Polexia Aphrodisia (Anna Paquin): Do you have any pot?

William Miller (Patrick Fugit): No. I'm a journalist.

Polexia Aphrodisia: Well, go do your job then. You're on the road, man. It's all happening! Get in there. Go talk to them!

—*ALMOST FAMOUS*

"Don't come up to me if you're not holding and go, 'Wanna get high?' 'cause I'll be like 'yeah,' and you'll go, 'me too,' and just stand there. I might head-butt you."

—BRIAN POSEHN

"Never *ever* narc."

—SETH MAXWELL MALICE, *DAZED AND CONFUSED* (BOOK)

"It's reverse psychology, okay? The undercover cop wants to look like a drug dealer. There's no way that guy's a cop because he looks so much like a cop. Think about it!"

—MICHAEL SHOWALTER ON *MICHAEL AND MICHAEL HAVE ISSUES*

"Here's the cash. Grab the stash."

—SETH ROGEN AS DALE DENTON, *PINEAPPLE EXPRESS*

Saul (James Franco): Herpes? . . . Do you know how many joints we've shared?

Red (Danny McBride): I know. I'm a disgusting person.

—*PINEAPPLE EXPRESS*

"How are we going to sell weed when we can't even water our lawns but twice a day. We're going to have the worst weed ever."

—WANDA SYKES

FINE FUMES: PINEAPPLE EXPRESS

Before the 2008 film, you were hard-pressed to come across any weed called Pineapple Express. Since the film, college freshmen and new stoners have been shelling out top dollar for hastily relabeled goods and then bragging about it on the Internet. That which we call a rose by any other name would smell as sweet, sure. But call it Pineapple Express, well, then people are going to go nutso and say it smells ten times better.

"Weed, you know, you just get mellow. You can drive pretty stoned and be OK. I mean, sometimes you get too stoned and you can't drive. But you could get pretty stoned and still drive."

—JASON MEWES

"If you do smoke marijuana, don't drive for at least a couple of hours; it's terribly important we show that we're responsible smokers."

—KEITH STROUP, NORML FOUNDER

"Just say to the folks, do not leave anything in here that wasn't in here when you got here."

—WHOOPI GOLDBERG ON *THE VIEW*

"No smoking and driving, bitches. Stay at the party!"

—DANNY DeVITO

"To the kids out there, stay away from drugs until you are old enough to make the decision wisely."

—SEN DOG OF CYPRESS HILL

POT SPOTS: CYPRESS HILL SMOKEOUT

"Californi-YEAH!" or . . . that's what you would say if you lived there. Billed as an all-day mind-opening music festival, this San Bernardino tradition outdid all other music festivals by allowing of-age state residents with their fun cards to light up in designated areas! And, those without cards may have been lucky enough to find a doctor in attendance. With bigger names performing every year (Incubus and MGMT in 2010), this music fest, like many Cali residents, is always growing.

"Learning to enjoy marijuana is a necessary but not a sufficient condition for a person to develop a stable pattern of drug use. He still has to contend with the powerful forces of social control that make the act seem inexpedient, immoral, or both."

—HOWARD S. BECKER, *MARI-JUANA USE AND THE SOCIAL CONTEXT*

"Stoned is stoned so don't be greedy."

—EVAN KELIHER, *GRANDPA'S MARIJUANA HANDBOOK*

CHAPTER 3

THE STONER'S KITCHEN

"Rice is great when you're hungry and you want two thousand of something."

—Mitch Hedberg

Dudes, look no further—your kitchen holds everything you need to get your best high. We're not all lucky enough to smoke from a Jerome Baker zong, but with some imagination, you can turn anything into a bong. Water bottles, coke cans, aluminum foil, apples—the world is your oyster, man. (Can you turn an oyster into a bong?) Or go ahead and just eat your stash. You could whip up some killer brownies or try your hand at magic pancakes. (You know Betty Crocker never tasted this good.) Seriously, a little creativity is all you need to get your ganja on, as the offerings in this chapter prove.

Todd (Allen Covert): This cake tastes a little funny.

John (Jonathan Loughran): Oh yeah, I dumped a fat sack of reefer into the mix. I thought I'd spice up the batch.

Mr. Beefy (Robert Smigel): Really?

Nicky (Adam Sandler): What's reefer?

Mr. Beefy: About five hundred bucks an ounce.

—LITTLE NICKY

"I'm especially looking forward to something called the 'munchies' phase where one enjoys bizarre food combinations. I'm thinking of pairing this Chilean sea bass with this aggressive Zinfandel."

—DAVID HYDE PIERCE AS NILES ON FRASIER

"Oh cool! Taco shells! They're like a little corn envelope—you know?"

—JON LOVITZ AS THE STONED GUY (STEVE) ON FRIENDS

"Is that a joint, man? Looks like a quarter-pounder, man."

—CHEECH MARIN AS PEDRO IN UP IN SMOKE

"Get some sour cream and onion chips with some dip, man, some beef jerky, some peanut butter. Get some Häagen-Dazs ice cream bars, a whole lot, make sure chocolate, gotta have chocolate, man. Some popcorn, red popcorn, graham crackers, graham crackers with marshmallows, the little marshmallows and little chocolate bars and we can make s'mores, man. . . . Also, celery, grape jelly, Cap'n Crunch with the little Crunch Berries, pizzas. We need two big pizzas, man, everything on 'em, with water, whole lotta water, and Funyons."

—JIM BREUER AS BRIAN, HALF BAKED

"In strict medical terms marijuana is far safer than many foods we commonly consume. For example, eating ten raw potatoes can result in a toxic response."

—DEA ADMINISTRATIVE LAW JUDGE FRANCIS L. YOUNG

"As I swallowed the last bite of the second cookie, the first cookie checked in like a velvet freight train."

—TOM DAVIS, THIRTY-NINE YEARS OF SHORT-TERM MEMORY LOSS

"Those lollipops, man. That's a smooth mellow high that lasts for hours."

—JOE ROGAN

"Maybe the lollipops went bad? I licked it. But somebody told me that you need to eat it. Somebody quite famous who grows his own, he told me I should be eating it. But at this point, I feel like 'Why bother?' I gave it a shot, it didn't work. I'm over it."

—MARY-LOUISE PARKER

"Usually one will feel the effects of bananadine after smoking three or four cigarettes."

—THE ANARCHIST COOKBOOK (BANANADINE, THE PSYCHOAC-TIVE COMPOUND IN BANANA PEELS, AS IT TURNS OUT, IS NOT REAL.)

"I consider it to be a misguided and potentially dangerous publication which should be taken out of print."

—WILLIAM POWELL, AUTHOR OF THE ANARCHIST COOKBOOK

"Oh, no thanks. I never touch the stuff. There's enough in the air here to get everybody high. Besides, it gives you the munchies. God knows I don't need that."

—CHRIS FARLEY AS MIKE DONNELLY, BLACK SHEEP

"He takes this brick of hash, whips out a knife, like Jesse James, and cuts me off a big slither. I go, 'Do you have a pipe to go with this?' And he handed me a Coke can."

—QUENTIN TARANTINO (ABOUT BRAD PITT)

"I rolled up twenty joints, put them in my Chesterfield pack, and started changing my habits."

—WILLIE NELSON

HIGH CREDENTIALS: WILLIE NELSON

"Free Willie!" cried the public, when Nelson was arrested at age seventy-seven for possession. Even the most conservative Americans were a bit vexed. It's Willie Nelson. He's earned the right. Let him (puff and) pass! Texas police clearly didn't understand that being Willie Nelson gives you the right to smoke up anytime anywhere. Since his arrest, Nelson has formed the Teapot Party, a movement to legalize his sweet bud and keep him out of jail when he is ninety.

"Baked, not fried . . . the healthy choice."

—CHRIS FERREIRA AS BILL IN GROOVE

"Gary was paranoid. He would take a knitting needle to his cigarettes, push out the smooth tobacco and replace it with weed. Whenever he wanted to partake, he'd just snap off the filter, roll the end and have a toke."

—DUSTIN DIAMOND, BEHIND THE BELL

"It's actually a Senegalese lute carved from deerwood, used for fertility rituals . . . Oh, and you can put your weed in there."

—ADAM SANDLER AS BONGO GUY, THE HOT CHICK

"We'll also provide you with a prescription bong. Do you want the wizard, or the skull?"

—HARRY SHEARER AS DR. HIBBERT, THE SIMPSONS

"I went to jail for it . . . nine months . . . for a bonnnnng. What were they thinking? 'Take away their bongs they won't be able to smoke their dope?' Hey, if we get a bud and get no way to smoke it, we turn into MacGyver in a heartbeat."

—TOMMY CHONG

"Remember that friend in high school who wanted to make bongs out of everything? Making bongs out of apples and oranges and shit. One day you find your friend goin' 'Hey look, man, I made a bong out of my head! Put the pot in this ear and suck it out of this one. Go on, take a hit!'"

—DENIS LEARY

McGayver Friend (Marc Cohen): Hey, man, we're out of papers.

McGayver Smoker (Stephen Baldwin): All right. Then get me a toilet paper roll, a corkscrew, and some tin foil.

McGayver Friend: We don't have a corkscrew.

McGayver Smoker: All right. Then get me an avocado, an ice pick, and my snorkel. Trust me, bro. I've made bongs with less. Hurry up!

—HALF BAKED

Thurgood Jenkins (Dave Chappelle): You know I got some weed at work today, if y'all wanna try it out.

Scarface (Guillermo Diaz): Nah, we don't feel like smokin' right now.

Thurgood Jenkins: Me neither. So y'all wanna smoke?

Scarface: I'll get Billy Bong Thornton!

—HALF BAKED

"When are you going to grow up? I don't want the twins keeping their money in a piggy bong the way that I did!"

—DAVID STRICKLAND AS TODD
ON SUDDENLY SUSAN

"I got papers, blunts, blongs, blokes, anything to make a high n*gga pie!"

—MARLON WAYANS AS SHORTY, SCARY MOVIE

"There are many options for those Trustafarians who choose . . . to use their financial backing to establish ganja status. Zongs are a type of glass bong that zig and zag their way to increased volume in a small amount of space while adding an architectural element that is reminiscent of a fun day at a water park."

—BRIAN GRIFFIN, THE TRUSTA-FARIAN HANDBOOK

"Pig Pen, when I want advice about a good *Planet of the Apes* film or maybe how to get the resin out of my bong I'll come to you, okay? But I am not gonna take romantic advice from somebody who cannot spell 'romantic' or 'advice' . . . or 'bong.'"

—JASON LONDON AS RICK IN OUT COLD

FINE FUMES: WHITE WIDOW
There's some insane resin action happening with this glittery grass. The White Widow is the rock candy of cannabis. Covered in icy crystals, this lady gets your whole body buzzin' and might take you on a little trip with her 15–20 percent THC. It's not clear how this widow got her name, but we're so glad she's single.

"A dope fiend refers to the reefer butt as a roach, because, it resembles a cockroach."

—MICHAEL JETER AS L. RON BUMQUIST IN FEAR AND LOATH-ING IN LAS VEGAS

"What the fuck are these people talking about? You'd have to be crazy on acid to think a joint looked like a goddamn cockroach!"

—BENICIO DEL TORO AS GONZO IN *FEAR AND LOATHING IN LAS VEGAS*

"I'm sophisticated enough now to know exactly what a roach is. It's half of a joint . . . it's what's left."

—DAWN WELLS, *THE VIEW*

"Every spliff is a roll-up but not every roll-up is a spliff."

—WAGNER CARRILHO, U.K. TV PERSONALITY

"What you do is you light all three ends at the same time, and then the smoke converges, creating a trifecta of joint-smoking power. This is it man, this is what your grandchildren are going to be smoking. The future."

—JAMES FRANCO AS SAUL SILVER, *PINEAPPLE EXPRESS* (READYING HIS CROSSROADS JOINT)

"Was the government to prescribe to us our medicine and diet, our bodies would be in such keeping as our souls are now."

—THOMAS JEFFERSON

FINE FUMES: FOUR-WAY

Three's company. Four's epic shit! You would think. There's little consensus about what a four-way strain actually is. To some it's a strain that does well in four different grow methods. Others claim it's a mix of four species of cannabis, but when you throw ruderalis in there it's probably not helping your high too much. Ask your pharmacists. We as a culture need to figure this one out.

"There are male and female plants. The substance that gives marijuana its famous psychoactive kick is concentrated in the flowers, or the buds, of the females. So when they're old enough to tell them apart, kill the males."

—PETER JENNINGS, POT OF GOLD, TV SPECIAL

"Your soil is what you make it."

—MOUNTAIN GIRL, PRIMO PLANT: GROWING MARIJUANA OUTDOORS

"That's a bad blend, it was harvested probably a year ago— and too soon. It's dried out, full of enough mold to cure strep."

—HUNTER PARRISH AS SILAS, WEEDS

"Nice little plant. You drink all this little water up so you can grow up to be a nice strong chronic plant. And then you'll be smoked by all the rappers and make them do a whole lot of dumb shit that fuck up their careers. Yes you will. Night-night, baby."

—MARLON WAYANS AS SHORTY,
SCARY MOVIE 2 (USING BONG
WATER ON HIS HERB)

FINE FUMES: SHAKE

Sometimes your dank is rank. This is not a pleasant option, but if you find yourself in a one-dealer town, this may be the shite you're stuck with. Shake is like Overstock.com or cheap tea bags: the things other companies couldn't sell get all mashed together and offered at a discount. So . . . sticks, damaged buds, stems . . . it's like a salad really, though it will get you a little high.

"Gerbils would produce a significant amount of CO_2 which would help plant growth. The extra oxygen would keep the gerbils energetic."

—ED ROSENTHAL,
THE BEST OF ASK ED

"During the first three or four weeks of flowering, seltzer water increases bud growth. After that, it is not a good idea to get the bud wet."

—ED ROSENTHAL,
THE BEST OF ASK ED

"It'll be okay. I'll fix my lasagna. We'll smoke a joint. Tensions will melt away."

—CAMERON DIAZ AS LOTTE IN
BEING JOHN MALKOVICH

"The Panama Red comes onto the market about the second week of April. This lasts for three months and then you get russet marijuana and after that red marijuana which is better than the russet but not as good as the spring."

—RICHARD NEVILLE,
PLAY POWER

Sookie (Claire Danes): You make it sound as if I'm anal or something, just because I know how to roll a perfect joint.

Igby (Kieran Culkin): No, not anal. Vegetarian.

Sookie: Well, what does that mean?

Igby: Well, you don't roll like, big Rasta spliff joints, do you? Your joints are like salad joints, not like a big, sloppy, bleeding cheeseburger-that-you-rip-into-kind-of-a-joint joint.

—*Igby Goes Down*

"I want you to take the Frankenstein shit, the deer shit, the green monster, the bling, and the bling bling, and I want you to roll it all into one joint."

—*Allen Covert as Alex in Grandma's Boy*

"My favorite kind of herb? Northern Lights. I like that shit that have me comatose—fall-asleep-with-the-blunt-in-my-hand-type shit."

—*Method Man*

"Today is Christmas cookie day. I thought, who could be better to make cookies than Snoop Dogg. And [to Snoop] you wanted us to make green-colored brownies."

—*Martha Stewart, The Martha Stewart Show*

"Pot brownies, baby. That's what it's all about. Makes it easy on travel day."

FINE FUMES: NORTHERN LIGHTS

In the "Drug Testing" episode of *The Office*, Dwight Schrute is narcing hardcore. He shows a photo of weed to Creed Bratton and asks him to ID it. Creed says it's "Northern Lights. *Cannabis indica*." Dwight says, "No. That's marijuana." Everyone is so in touch! Northern Lights is an award-winning strain, a hybrid, but mostly indica, as Wacky Weed Creed is well aware.

"I'm trying to bake some brownies, but we missing the most important part of the brownies."

—SNOOP DOGG, *THE MARTHA STEWART SHOW*

"I learned how to make a pot brownie. I went on Google. But then I realized the people who put up the recipes are stoners and they were writing a lot about the planet before they actually gave out the recipe. I made them and fell asleep. They should put them in a bottle and manufacture them instead of sleeping pills."

—JOHN MAYER

"Nance, trust me. A bakery is virtually impossible to run without drug money."

—KEVIN NEALON AS DOUG WILSON ON *WEEDS*

"Labeling must include a warning if nuts or other known allergens are used, and must include the total weight (in ounces or grams) of cannabis in the package. A warning that the item is a medication and not a food must be distinctly and clearly legible on the front of the package."

—SAN FRANCISCO PUBLIC HEALTH DEPARTMENT OFFICIAL MEMO

"I think they should say that 'this was baked by a nut.' The city of San Francisco is ruled by absolutely insane Marxists."

—MICHAEL SAVAGE

"We weren't buying, like, twenty-dollar jumbos; we were paying money, we were buying, like, an ounce. . . . We weren't doing, like, pipe smoking, we didn't get that far. You put your marijuana, you lace it (with cocaine), you roll it up and you smoke it in your weed. . . . It's almost like heroin and cocaine speedballing, but you level it off with the marijuana."

—WHITNEY HOUSTON

HIGH CREDENTIALS: WHITNEY HOUSTON
Never underestimate Houston's talents. After being caught with about half an ounce of weed at a Hawaiian airport, she simply walked away and boarded a commercial flight to Los Angeles, somehow (masterfully) eluding the airport security. Being a celebrity has some dope ass perks!

"'How'd you get your names?' We used to wear little bags around our necks was called a 'grouch bag.' In this bag, we would keep our pennies, our marbles, piece of candy, little marijuana, whatever you could think of. Well we were studying to be musicians. Groucho got his name from the bag."

—CHICO MARX, SHOWTIME (BBC)

"We kept our marijuana in a Prince Albert tin."

—ETTA JAMES, RAGE TO SURVIVE

> ## "The first thing that I smoked out of was a tinnie in maybe seventh or eighth grade."
>
> —ASHER ROTH, RAPPER

"Did you see me last year? Have a look at last year. Yep. Year of the Munchie 2009. Weed, it's such a lovely drug. It is such a lovely drug. But it doesn't mix well with me—at all."

—ROBBIE WILLIAMS

"Pot butter is a butter substitute and can be used in anything in which butter is used, taking its exalted place, perched high above the food pyramid."

—BRIAN GRIFFIN, *THE TRUSTA-FARIAN HANDBOOK*

KG (Kyle Gass): Go score me a dime-bag.

JB (Jack Black): A what?

KG: Ten dollars worth of weed. Now listen: Go down to Wake & Bake Pizza; ask for Jojo. Tell him you want the Bob Marley Extra Crispy. He'll know what you're talkin' about.

—TENACIOUS D IN THE PICK OF DESTINY

"Recipe for failure: take one part natural talent, two parts stellar education, mix with easy success and a generous helping of booze, drugs, and women, and immediately set on fire."

—BRADLEY COOPER AS JACK BOURDAIN IN *KITCHEN CONFIDENTIAL*

"Many kids can tell you about drugs but do not know what celery or courgettes taste like."

—JAMIE OLIVER (IT WILL HELP
TO KNOW A COURGETTE IS A
ZUCCHINI.)

"I remember one time [my wife] Patricia was learning how to make my mom's special spaghetti sauce. My mom came over to our house and showed Patricia her secret ingredient . . . a 'stash' of herbs. . . . Patricia had never seen oregano before and in her astonishment she thought, 'Oh, my god, Tony's mom uses pot in his favorite recipe!'"

—TONY BENNETT,
THE GOOD LIFE

"Hey, Mom! It's me, Jerri. It's not so bad making friends with drugs, is it? I mean, come on, it always worked before. In the old days, I would turn people on to hash, or Thai stick or a palm-full of goofballs or 'ludes. God, they don't make those anymore. Or, oh, sometimes, this would do the trick: Stoney and I would go over to Buckle's and Puff would turn us on to a hot load of mescaline crumbled into a tumbler of ether with a float of Percocet jimmies. Mmm! I'd wake up with blood on my ass and then we'd get high. God, those were some good times. Mmm!"

—AMY SEDARIS AS JERRI BLANK
ON *STRANGERS WITH CANDY*

"I really don't see anything wrong with [weed]. I wish there was a healthy, legal way to do it where you could eat it or something."

—AFROMAN

"Well, I have heard that chocolate has some of the same elements that marijuana does. And marijuana presumably makes people happy. Chocolate certainly does."

—JULIA CHILD

CHAPTER 4

BUZZ KILLERS

"The devastating insights achieved when high are real insights."

—Carl Sagan

We're smoking up for a reason: We would like things to seem a little bit better than they are. Or, we want to be popular, but it's mostly to improve situations, to relax, to enjoy, to enlighten, to buzz.

And when that goes wrong, it's just the worst! Not only are you out four dubs and in one major bummer, you also wasted all the energy you put into acquiring the weed and not getting caught. *And* to top it off, you now run the risk of getting paranoid that this negative will repeat itself on future attempts. It's the same with dudes' erections: You lose one and it's hard to pull out of that downward spiral— well, actually it's depressingly easy to pull out at that point.

With all the effort and funds you put into getting this opportunity, you deserve your buzz. Learn here, from others' experiences, what to avoid to keep it.

"What no one ever explained is that the way marijuana enables you to forget your problems is one hundred percent addictive. The drug itself may not be addictive, but if you've got things bothering you, as I did, you're going to get hooked on whatever helps you to shove them aside. And I was someone who had problems."

—DREW BARRYMORE, *LITTLE GIRL LOST*

"The novelty experience generator is tired. . . . The aftereffects of pot are the loss of edge, the diminishing of optimal performance."

—TIMMEN L. CERMAK, MD, *MARIJUANA: WHAT'S A PARENT TO BELIEVE?*

"I was very open about smoking pot. I got away with it until [John] Belushi died. That was the end of that. I couldn't smoke in the office openly anymore. No more of that shit. As long as we were a hot show, I felt I could get away with it. But when Belushi died, and then everyone started having babies, that was the end."

—TOM DAVIS, *LIVE FROM NEW YORK: AN UNCENSORED HISTORY OF SATURDAY NIGHT LIVE*

Desmond's Mother (Tyra Ferrell): You're a smart boy, Roy. So why are you doing a stupid thing like drugs? Hmm?

Roy (Leonardo Nam): Err . . . something to do.

—*THE PERFECT SCORE*

"The fact that you add adrenaline into it, that you have to hide and there's shame, actually can make it feel more addictive. It can make it more dangerous."

—JULIE HOLLAND, MD

"I've stopped smoking weed with black people. . . . Every time I smoke weed with my black friends, all you talk about is your trials and your tribulations. . . . I'm smoking weed to run away from my problems, not take on yours."

—DAVE CHAPPELLE

"There are very serious beauty issues at stake here. Number one: smoking pot takes the moisture right out your skin. Number two: it can leave you with premature crow's feet from going like this (taking a puff, squinting, smoky titter)."

—ANGELA WATSON AS KAREN, STEP BY STEP

"I thought that marijuana was helping me with my panic attacks by mellowing me out, but I had actually been encouraging panic attacks with each toke."

—JAY MOHR, GRASPING FOR AIRTIME

"I would never get high before a show. Because when I'm high, I don't want to stand in front of a bunch of people I don't know. That does not sound comfortable."

—MITCH HEDBERG

"I'm no longer necessary. I'm in the way. . . . My plans are to figure out some new identity. I'm gonna have to kill off one life and start another one."

—HUNTER S. THOMPSON, OMNIBUS

HIGH CREDENTIALS: MITCH HEDBERG

You can tell Hedberg had some amazing highs. This comedian's jokes were just far enough from reality that they took an extra beat to appreciate, and luckily for us—his far-from-reality audience—his slow and mellow delivery allowed us the time to do it. His CDs, DVDs, and YouTube clips survive him and are the perfect complement to any packed bowl.

"We had a number of accidental deaths while I was over there and it wouldn't surprise me if some of those 'accidental' deaths were possibly caused by some GIs being scared under combat conditions because of marijuana."

—Jackie Robinson sr.,
I Never Had It Made

"This is all I'm going to say about drugs. Stay away from them. There's a time and a place for everything, and it's called college."

—Isaac Hayes as Chef, *South Park*

"I was going to go make a film in Greece and in Greece, if they caught you with this much marijuana, they threw you in jail, no questions asked, and I was trying to stuff it in my deodorant bottles, you know, in the bottom of my deodorant because I thought they'll never look in there. And I thought, what I am doing? Is this thing bigger than me? Yes, well, I need help with it."

—Dyan Cannon

"'Uh oh,' I thought, 'I've toked up. Does this mean now I'm a loser?'"

—Dustin Diamond,
Behind the Bell

"If I smoke really powerful weed, I get paranoid and nonverbal."

—JACK BLACK

"I haven't tried pot because I know the second I'd light one up Janet Reno would kick my door down—she'd do it too!"

—CANDICE BERGEN AS MURPHY BROWN ON *MURPHY BROWN*

"I always wanted to blunt and blur what was painful. My idea was pain reduction and mind expansion, but I ended up with mind reduction and pain expansion."

—CARRIE FISHER

"I've been jailed in eight out of ten provinces."

—MARC EMERY

"I found a bag of pot in your underwear drawer, and you told me that you thought they were pencil shavings."

—JOSEPH BOLOGNA AS LENNY IN *BIG DADDY*

"What, do you think we're a bunch of idiots? You want us to believe you're all of a sudden in the marijuana storage business?"

—TIM ALLEN AS TIM TAYLOR ON *HOME IMPROVEMENT* (IN RESPONSE TO THE TIMELESS "I'M HOLDING IT FOR A FRIEND.")

"I certainly had my day; now it just kinda turns me into a doughnut."

—BRAD PITT

"Yeah, marijuana just did a real reverse on me. It would have been great if I'd liked that, but it made me—you know, to say self-conscious doesn't do it justice—paranoid, and very unhappy."

—CARRIE FISHER

"When I have seven-eighths of a gram of marijuana, I consider myself to be out of marijuana."

—RON WHITE

"It doesn't affect me anymore. There's so much THC in my system, nothing happens."

—MARGARET CHO

"At the onset it was all giggles and munchies and floating in a friendly haze—it suddenly became creepy and dark and scary."

—CARRIE FISHER, WISHFUL DRINKING

"I'm like a comedian, so if I get a laugh from a person who's high, it doesn't count, you know, 'cause they're always laughing."

—WOODY ALLEN AS ALVY IN ANNIE HALL

"I had friends who were young intellectuals who broke company with me because I was smoking it. They refused to see me. They felt about it, I think, the way people felt in London in 1890 about taking opium."

—NORMAN MAILER

"Marijuana is . . . self-punishing. It makes you acutely sensitive, and in this world, what worse punishment could there be?"

—P. J. O'ROURKE

"My lungs—I smoked so much, I'd roll 'em and smoke 'em and roll 'em and smoke 'em—I did get congestion from it."

—WILLIE NELSON

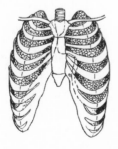

"Yoga and smoking a joint are very similar things. One, you take the elevator to the top floor, and the other you climb up the mountain. But the one gives you ultimately a deficit, whereas the yoga continually pays dividends."

—WOODY HARRELSON

"The longer you hold it in, the more you feel it. . . . You're going to be high for the next two to three hours, unless you eat. If you eat the high is gone in five minutes . . . with vapor especially."

—EAGLE BILL, CHEROKEE MARIJUANA MEDICINE MAN

FINE FUMES: ABV WEED

In case you want to try killing your vapor high by eating, maybe use some ABV for that munching. ABV stands for "Already been vaporized." Your weed is ready to go a second round, often maintaining an impressive amount of potency. So, always save it to savor it! Use it for cooking, just like when your cheap-ass friend brings you a bottle of something called "red table wine."

"If you're Jewish, do not smoke weed and go to the Anne Frank house. That is a terrible combination; you will think the Nazis are after you."

—DAN LEVY, COMEDIAN

POT SPOTS: CUZCO, PERU

It's not hard to score your indica in this Inca capital. If you like your smoke chased or laced with coke, then this is the toke town for you. It's a stoned-throw from beautiful (extra beautiful when blazed) Machu Picchu, so be sure to take a trip there too.

"There was a negative air in the room which made me want to vomit. I like to be around the happy air."

—SHANNON HOON OF BLIND MELON

"If I had to get trapped inside something, I'd rather it be a guitar or even a temporary marijuana haze than in a video game, and certainly not in a computer."

—JEFF BRIDGES

"At every big party I'd go to, people were high on something. Cocaine flowed as freely as champagne, and soon I began joining in the festivities. . . . Compounded with my pot smoking, the whole thing started sneaking up on me."

—TONY BENNETT, *THE GOOD LIFE*

"Researchers tested a new form of medical marijuana that treats pain but doesn't get the user high, prompting patients who need medical marijuana to declare, 'Thank you?'"

—JIMMY FALLON

"Because I'm a young black man driving a really nice, expensive car, I sometimes get harassed when I'm rolling through a ghetto neighborhood. The cops don't know who I am right away—their first thought is, 'That must be a dope dealer or some kind of gangster. . . . Let's go see.'"

—COOLIO

"I've had a select set of really beautiful, powerful, psychedelic experiences on certain drugs but I never got into just doing it at a party: 'Oh let's get fucked up and drop acid.' That's so retarded and disrespectful to your body and the drug itself. Mushrooms, acid, and ecstasy can offer you a new perspective. They can also offer you nothing."

—JOSEPH GORDON-LEVITT

"If the milk turns out to be sour, I ain't the type of pussy to drink it."

—VAS BLACKWOOD AS RORY BREAKER IN *LOCK, STOCK AND TWO SMOKING BARRELS*

J (Nicholas Rowe): I've a strong suspicion we should have been rocket scientists, or Nobel Peace Prize winners or something.
Charles (Nick Marcq): Peace Prize? Ooh. Be lucky to find your penis for a piss, the amount you keep smoking."

—*LOCK, STOCK AND TWO SMOKING BARRELS*

"I've got no one. No friends, no family. Nobody. It's just me. Just me and my ganja."

—LAURIE METCALF AS JACKIE HARRIS ON *ROSEANNE*

"The more I heard about how even a small infraction follows someone for the rest of their lives, and [marijuana] has become such a prevalent use in society, it seemed like an unfair tag to stick on somebody."

—AZAR NAFISI, IRANIAN WRITER

Tom DeLonge: Mark, can I tell you what I was thinking? I was thinking that you and I and Travis are giving it everything we got and then there are people here smoking marijuana!

Mark Hoppus: It's going to give us tiny testicles!

—BLINK 182 (A JOKE!)

"Sometimes it's not even the drugs that'll kill you man. What really kills you is looking for drugs."

—TOMMY CHONG AS HIMSELF IN *THINGS ARE TOUGH ALL OVER*

"Despair is a narcotic. It lulls the mind into indifference."

—CHARLIE CHAPLIN AS HENRI VERDOUX IN *MONSIEUR VERDOUX*

"I'm disappointed that [the Marijuana Party] is, in fact, running candidates. Unfortunately, they're all eccentrics, typically, and they're all doing it for alternative reasons—and can't possibly provide any benefit to the marijuana community by running."

—MARC EMERY, CANADIAN "PRINCE OF POT"

HIGH CREDENTIALS: MARC EMERY
One of the most renowned stoners in the word, "Prince of Pot," and publisher of *Cannabis Culture* magazine, Canadian Marc Emery is currently serving a five-year prison sentence in Georgia (U.S.A.) for selling those most insidious of nature's weapons: seeds. He's also serving as a reminder that nothing good lasts forever. Canada, once the United States' really cool upstairs neighbor, is growing up into a cranky landlord, evicting one of its best citizens.

"Life's a tradeoff. It's finally legal to smoke dope, but you got to have cancer."

—SUSAN SARANDON AS JACKIE HARRISON IN *STEPMOM*

"I've gone for months without smoking pot and I'm used to it."

—MARC EMERY (ON HIS JAIL SENTENCE: MAJOR BUZZ KILL)

CHAPTER 5

BUZZ ENHANCERS

"Energy comes out of the outlets into our amplifiers, and then the energy comes off us and it goes into the audience, and they bounce it back. We just play catch with some vibes."

—Kurt Cobain

What goes well with weed? Everything that wasn't in the last chapter. And after those buzz killers, it is time to bring on some smiles, dudes. The list of cannabis complements is pretty epic! Tennis, Pringles, banging someone, Otto Dix, doing the laundry, *Fallout 3*, craft beers, the pasta section of a grocery store, the Wookie language, a mirror! There are lots of ways to elevate your high even higher. Not all of them are safe, so use your judgment. For instance, commuting to work on a riding mower while you're stoned is an amazing experience. It's just not recommended. Let's see what other "recommendations" those in the know about the grow have.

"Music and herb go together. It's been a long time now I smoke herb from 1960s, when I first start singing."

—Bob Marley

"I love guitar, especially when I'm smoking."

—Julian Marley

"I get on my high plane. I turn on my Metallica."

—Jim Breuer

"It's like my tightrope walk. I get fucked up then play hella guitar. That's my stunt. . . . Watch me smoke this and do this."

—Afroman

"[Louis] Armstrong had endless energy and could play and play and play with the evangelical fire and charisma that brings a new art into being."

—Stanley Crouch

"The song 'Legalize It,' from the album of the same name, became an anthem and a rally cry across the globe."

—Dave Tosh (about dad Peter's song)

"Herb make you control yourself. Herb make you endure bad things. . . . Herb make you be calm."

—Bob Marley

"I'll smoke some pot for you here. It is a nice kind of deep orange and almost turquoise California weed. That should calm you down; you'll get a contact buzz."

—Hunter S. Thompson, quoted in Sausage Factory: The College Crier's Infamous Interviews of the Freaks and the Famous (phone interview)

"The biggest killer on the planet is stress, and I still think the best medicine is and always has been cannabis."

—WILLIE NELSON

"It makes me much more enthusiastic about things that I actually enjoy doing, so it doesn't, like, take away your motivation. It'll just take away your motivation to do something that fucking sucks."

—JOE ROGAN

"Facing reality is easier when you are high."

—JACKIE ROBINSON SR., *I NEVER HAD IT MADE*

"We found the hippie holy grail, a government-sponsored dope store that served tea and snacks."

—TOM DAVIS, *THIRTY-NINE YEARS OF SHORT-TERM MEMORY LOSS*

Annie (Diane Keaton): Well, have you ever made love high?

Alvy (Woody Allen): Me? No. You know, if I have grass or alcohol or anything, I get unbearably wonderful. I get too, too wonderful for words."

—*ANNIE HALL*

"I have always loved marijuana. It has been a source of joy and comfort to me for many years. And I still think of it as a basic staple of life, along with beer and ice and grapefruits—and millions of Americans agree with me."

—HUNTER S. THOMPSON

"I love weed, *love it*! Probably always will! But not as much as I love pussy! The end."

—DAVE CHAPPELLE AS THURGOOD JENKINS IN *HALF BAKED*

"I smoked a little grass. I can't do this job without it, I need it to relax."

—Nigel Kennedy, Classical Musician

"I smoked a long time. . . . It's a thousand times better than whiskey. . . . It's an assistant—a friend."

—Louis Armstrong

"It's true that marijuana is a fantastically effective aphrodisiac, and the person who understands pot can weave together a symphony of visual, auditory, olfactory, gustatory, tactual sensitivity to make lovemaking and adventure which dwarfs the imagination of the pornographers."

—Timothy Leary

POT SPOTS: OAHU
There is a real Pineapple Express, and it can be found on the Dole Plantation on Oahu. This scenic train ride has been sending honeymooners to their divorce lawyers faster than, well, not much. At six miles per hour, this tour of pineapple fields might require you to be stoned to enjoy it.

"Okay, let's see, toke as needed. Caution: objects may seem more edible than they actually are."

—Dan Castellaneta as Homer Simpson on *The Simpsons*

"Is listening to Pink Floyd in the dark a medical condition?"

—JON STEWART, *THE DAILY SHOW*

"What we've been doing lately is smoking massive amounts of drugs, binging on Entenmann's and listening to old Pink Floyd CDs."

—NATALIE PORTMAN AS MARTY IN *BEAUTIFUL GIRLS*

"jumping into shower.going to spend my afternoon playing World Of Warcraft butt naked&stoned. Perfect Sunday!"

—ADRIANNE CURRY, MODEL/TV PERSONALITY, VIA TWITTER

"The best antidote for excess adrenaline, in my humble but experienced opinion, is pot! Marijuana, hemp, weed, da kind, whatever you want to call it. You see, pot actually counters the effects of adrenaline because it slows you down."

—TOMMY CHONG, *CHEECH AND CHONG: THE UNAUTHORIZED AUTOBIOGRAPHY*

"Quit worrying, Brennan, that's what the weed is for."

—MICHAEL ZEGEN AS ERIC, *ADVENTURELAND*

"I felt so high after leaving the voting booth since I never thought I would be able to vote for this issue."

—RUTH BEAZER, *MY LIFE AS A CULTIVATED WEED*

"He was high—in that marijuana glow where the world relaxes."

—MALCOLM X, *THE AUTOBIOGRAPHY OF MALCOLM X* (OF A WHITE BOY IN A SPEAKEASY)

"The illegality of cannabis is outrageous, an impediment to full utilization of a drug which helps produce the serenity and insight, sensitivity and fellowship so desperately needed in this increasingly mad and dangerous world."

—CARL SAGAN

"Seeing an aura around objects is somewhat more common in the Younger group than in the Older group."

—CHARLES T. TART, PHD, ON BEING STONED

"It makes everything better. Makes food taste better, makes music better, makes sex feel better for God sakes. It makes shitty movies better, you know?"

—SETH ROGEN AS DALE DENTON, PINEAPPLE EXPRESS

"Laundry is great when you're high!"

—SARAH SILVERMAN (MAYBE LAURA SILVERMAN, WHO WAS JUST OFFSCREEN)

"This is like if that Blue Oyster shit met that Afghan Kush I had and they had a baby. And then, meanwhile, that crazy Northern Light stuff I had and the Super Red Espresso Snowflake met and had a baby, and by some miracle, those two babies met and fucked, this would be the shit that they birthed."

—JAMES FRANCO AS SAUL, PINEAPPLE EXPRESS

FINE FUMES: THAI STICK

Thai Stick is a classic handicraft among stoners, very popular in the 1960s and '70s, but much like its contemporary, the pet rock, when more potent forms of amusement were born, the novelty of these wrapped skewers of buds was quickly lost.

"I liked the drama of getting stoned."

—BRION JAMES, ACTOR

"If college kids find this entertaining, they must be on drugs!"

—RICHARD ROEPER (REVIEWING *THE SPONGEBOB SQUAREPANTS MOVIE*)

"I like the mellow vibe of herb, its uninhibiting effect. For me, it's a better drug than any of the others, and since we're all drug addicts, I don't think it's a bad choice. Whether your drug is sugar, coffee, sex, exercise, or religion—everybody has something."

—WOODY HARRELSON

"I've been smoking pot all my life. I've found it tremendously relaxing. I do it a lot. The doctor told me, 'Don't smoke cigarettes. Just smoke pot.'"

—RODNEY DANGERFIELD, *LIVE FROM NEW YORK: AN UNCENSORED HISTORY OF SATURDAY NIGHT LIVE*

"*Weeds* was my solace and respite in the back of the bus on tour. I was in the middle of detoxing at the time, and it was my replacement addiction for food. *Weeds* helps me. The irony is hilarious."

—ALANIS MORISSETTE

"Sophomore year I tried marijuana and fell completely in love with it. I went home and watched *Love Connection* and was like, 'Ooooohhhh man . . .' You know?"

—CHRIS FARLEY, *THE CHRIS FARLEY SHOW: A BIOGRAPHY IN THREE ACTS*

"I like any reaction I can get with my music. Just anything to get people to think. I mean if you can get a whole room full of drunk, stoned people to actually wake up and think, you're doing something."

—JIM MORRISON

"In no way does this mean that we at 'Weekend Update' advocate the smoking of marijuana. It's just that a survey shows that 90 percent of our viewers smoke it daily."

—DAN AYKROYD ON *SATURDAY NIGHT LIVE*

"That's how the Dead influenced me. And there's something magical about transcribing a solo played by someone who's stoned out of their mind. . . . To this day, when I hear 'Dark Star' I feel a little high!"

—WILL RAY

Alvy (Woody Allen): With your wife in bed, does she need some kind of artificial stimulation, like, like marijuana?
Old Man on Street (Albert Ottenheimer): We use a large vibrating egg.

—*ANNIE HALL*

"We always got a strong response, but I think in this day and age there is less of a marijuana fog at concerts and more of people just more naturally exuberant—it seems to me."

—JAMES YOUNG OF STYX

"Marijuana enhances many things, colors, flavors, sensations, but you are certainly not fucking empowered. When you're stoned, you're lucky if you can find your own goddamn feet. The only way it's a performance-enhancing drug is if there's a big fucking Hershey bar at the end of the run. Then you'll be like a Swiss ski jumper going, 'I'm there!'"

—ROBIN WILLIAMS IN *ROBIN WILLIAMS: LIVE ON BROADWAY*

"Many artists and writers have used cannabis for creative stimulation—from the writers of the world's religious masterpieces to our most irreverent satirists."

—JACK HERER

"I'm trying to go everywhere and have as much fun as I can, just singing from my heart—singing best I can—and these vegetables help me do just that."

—AFROMAN

"[*Tenacious D*] was always just a fun thing that we could do, to go out and blow people's minds with our ridiculousness. It was very much cardboard-box-and-duct-tape-style entertainment. Butt-flap, I guess is what you'd call it. Butt-flap theater. And it's still that. I still look forward to partying with Kyle and doing dumb and interesting stuff."

—JACK BLACK

"The coke, weed, acid, crystal meth, alcohol, and whatever pills I could get my hands on kept my mind in a haze. They allowed me to not think, which I needed, because when I had time to think bad things happened."

—KENDRA WILKINSON, *SLIDING INTO HOME*

"When I was high, I just *had* to drive a car. It is a great bit of good fortune that I never hit any living beings."

—GRACE SLICK, ROCK SINGER, SOMEBODY TO LOVE

"Even though I never loved getting high—food has always been my addiction—I joined in. And Brad seemed to enjoy it so much—certainly sex was better when we were both high."

—SUSAN BLUESTEIN DAVIS, AFTER MIDNIGHT: THE LIFE AND DEATH OF BRAD DAVIS

"I'd get up in the morning, wake and bake, watch MTV, sing along with the Buggles, play some guitar, take a nap, and get on with the day. No harm, no foul."

—DAVE MUSTAINE OF MEGADETH, MUSTAINE: A HEAVY METAL MEMOIR

"I was told by many people that if I smoked a lot of grass I could hear a lot of chords. My reply, and it was honest, I would say, I can't even hear the ones I play now."

—BARNEY KESSEL, JAZZ GUITARIST, SWING TO BOP

"There's only room for one Mary in my life . . . Mary Lane. With an 'L'! For love! I love Mary Lane!"

—CHRISTIAN CAMPBELL AS JIMMY IN REEFER MADNESS: THE MOVIE MUSICAL

"I remember smoking marijuana then because I hadn't in a long time and it makes you dance, gives you a terrific looseness. We were smoking Thai sticks and you'd dance for hours."

—TRUMAN CAPOTE, CONVERSATIONS WITH CAPOTE

POT SPOTS: MAINE

Maine was the first state to ban alcohol and start that nonsense tradition of prohibition, but it's come a long way since. Certainly sharing most of its border with Canada helped. Stephen King touts the local crops, and for sure, the East Coast Portland doesn't disappoint. Also, if you're into lobster dipped in pot butter, Maine may become your new home.

Cheech (Cheech Marin): Man, I can't believe you. Every time you do coke this shit happens.

Chong (Tommy Chong): Hey, wait a minute, man, how come every time I do coke you say that "every time you do coke" thing?

—*NICE DREAMS*

CHAPTER 6

THE HIGH LIFE

"We were just unknown young actors in L.A. I even remember his little bungalow that we lived in off Melrose that we'd smoke lots of pot in. Then we split, and he became Brad Pitt."

—Juliette Lewis

A paparazzo snaps a shot of Charlize Theron or Johnny Depp taking a hit from a granny smith in the privacy of their own backyard, and part of you is miffed—leave 'em alone! But another part of you is stoked. At least you have one thing in common with really rich Hollywood celebrities.

You know that smoking up isn't limited to just crusty couches in low-light apartments, but did you know that the high life can be glamorous?

Think about it. *Someone* is buying those gold-plated luxury hookahs out there. If it's not you, here are some quotes that just may inspire you to pursue a life of Panama Red carpets and Megan Fox's house parties.

"I want to smoke pot, but I can't. I'm too paranoid."

—DREW BARRYMORE (YET SHE WAS SEEN PUFFING AND PASSING WITH BUD CAMERON DIAZ)

"I'm a dad now. You want to be alert and my eyes used to glaze over when I did that."

—BRAD PITT

"I enjoy it once in a while. There's nothing wrong with it, everything in moderation. I wouldn't call myself a pot head."

—JENNIFER ANISTON

"I think pot should be legal. I don't smoke it, but I like the smell of it."

—ANDY WARHOL

"I'm going to make an admission, and I hope you're all sitting down. . . . I have smoked weed."

—WHOOPI GOLDBERG

"I'm not a great pothead or anything like that. I might socially have a couple of drinks here and there, but weed is much, much less dangerous than alcohol."

—JOHNNY DEPP

"I wouldn't call it recreational drug use, because it makes it sounds like I'm going to clubs and doing cocaine and things like that."

—MEGAN FOX

"I smoked marijuana and it gave me a perception, which I thought was real, true. But now I realize you can get to that heightened state of consciousness without drugs."

—GABRIEL BYRNE

"I'm not some chick on the road getting high and fucked up every night. I wake up, drink coffee, and get on the phone to talk about the creative direction of the next video."

—LADY GAGA

THE QUOTABLE STONER

"Suddenly, I felt like I was wearing patchouli in a room full of Chanel."

—SARAH JESSICA PARKER AS CARRIE BRADSHAW ON *SEX AND THE CITY*

FINE FUMES: PATCHOULI

Some people wear patchouli oil just to smell nice, but most are using it to cover up the scent of sensimilla. On the other hand, some are just hiding the fact they haven't showered. Approach with caution.

"I don't smoke pot anymore. I just pay a dude fifty bucks to come over, press lightly on my chest and tell me all my ideas are awesome."

—JOHN MAYER

"I wanted to try several things and make an informed decision, but I didn't enjoy anything other than marijuana. I don't even think of it as a drug—it should be legalized."

—MEGAN FOX

"Snoop was a year older than me. He stood out. He was tall and skinny and wore ponytails all over his head. I'm sure I probably bought weed from him."

—CAMERON DIAZ

"I smoke weed all day. I'm a very successful addict. And a smart one. And a very charismatic one."

—LIL WAYNE

"[I use marijuana] every single day, and I will do so every day, until the day I drop dead."

—MONTEL WILLIAMS

"I can't tell you how much bullshit I've been through because I will openly say that I smoke weed. People look at it like it's this crazy, hippie, fucked-up thing to do. And it's not!"

—MEGAN FOX

FINE FUMES: OPTIMUS PRIME

Not just an on-screen ally to Megan Fox, this is a hybrid strain (BC Sweet Tooth and Mayne Island Indica) that gives you an all-around high, but it's really featured here because of the sweet name. Stoners are lucky. We have dazzling scientists and farmers who can play with genetics and still have laidback whatevs to name their creations after a Transformer.

"It's more of a herb. I don't regret saying that at all. I think everyone smokes weed and people who say they don't are lying."

—Joss Stone

"Michael Vick, really? You didn't want to throw your weed away before you went through security. Really. You have 117 million dollars left on your contract. You know what 117 million dollars means? You can afford to replace your weed if you have to throw it away at the airport. Really."

—Seth Meyers on Saturday Night Live

"I don't know anyone who hasn't smoked dope. I don't anymore. I can't afford to be that spacey anymore."

—Patti Davis, daughter of President Ronald and Nancy Reagan

"I think hard drugs are disgusting, but I must say, I think marijuana is pretty lightweight."

—Linda McCartney

"It's always been my responsibility. If it was Hollywood to blame, then we'd all be dope addicts."

—CARRIE FISHER

"Instead of taking five or six of the prescriptions, I decided to go a natural route and smoke marijuana."

—MELISSA ETHERIDGE

HIGH CREDENTIALS: MELISSA ETHERIDGE

Etheridge gets credit for bringing a celebrity face and scalp to the idea that marijuana can really be used and not abused as medicine. When seriously harsh cancer treatments threatened to take away the use of her guitar-strummin' fingers, she decided to make the switch to a friendly weed. Pretty soon she was out on stage at the 2005 Grammy Awards, rocking out to "Piece of My Heart," in tribute to Janis Joplin.

"People give me pot all the time."

—MARY-LOUISE PARKER

HIGH CREDENTIALS: MARY-LOUISE PARKER

Parker isn't a stoner. She gave pot a shot, and it just wasn't her thing. That's fine. We don't just like her character Nancy Botwin on *Weeds*, we like her because she's like a cool mom: informed and not judgmental, a great role model for the nonstoners of the world. And also, she seems tough, like someone you'd be afraid to fight or write about negatively.

"You know how I feel about things, right? I wanna know about the things before I do them."

—OLIVIA MUNN,
ATTACK OF THE SHOW!

"[Tupac] always wanted me to smoke weed with him, and I never did it, and I wish I did. That's my biggest regret."

—MIKE TYSON

"I was asked to sing about killing, to sing about ass-kicking, to sing about getting high. It would have been the easiest thing in the world for me to write about marijuana. After all, I was a pothead; I knew its effects. I could have written a thesis about marijuana if I'd wanted to. But that didn't interest me."

—VICO C, RAPPER

"Opium and hash and pot—now—those things aren't drugs; they just bend your mind a little. I think everybody's mind should be bent once in a while."

—BOB DYLAN

"I don't think smoking the occasional spliff is all that wrong. I'd rather my son did it in front of me than behind closed doors."

—SIR RICHARD BRANSON

"Never give up the ganja."

—MORGAN FREEMAN (WHEN ASKED ABOUT HIS SMOKING HABITS)

"I was sixteen when I went to prison but he's been busted a couple of times. He should get a driver or go to Amsterdam where pot is legal."

—MARK WAHLBERG
(ON GEORGE MICHAEL)

POT SPOTS: AMSTERDAM

You always assured your mom you were going to visit the Anne Frank house. Lies! You were there for the whores and the cafes where you can get easy breezy weed. And you had a great time! Next time though, check out the Anne Frank house. It's a bummer, but so interesting.

"I think that everybody in the media world and in the sports world knows that NBA players do smoke marijuana."

—Josh Howard of the Dallas Mavericks

"I don't have a stance on it. I enjoy it . . . not while I'm pregnant, obviously."

—Alanis Morissette

"I was wilding out and shit, but I'm good now. I just smoke weed. I know n*ggers die when they twenty-seven. I'm twenty-six now, but I promise I'll live 'til I'm old as shit."

—Kid Cudi

"Robert Mitchum [was] then thought to be a dangerous guy, because he had once been busted on a marijuana rap."

—Richard Schickel, film critic and documentarian, Mitchum: In His Own Words

"The only difference between me and my fellow actors is that I've spent more time in jail."

—Robert Mitchum

"I'd won a Stony Award for best actress—my second year winning it, by the way. They never did give me another trophy. I wonder if they were too high and just forgot to make them. It's a great trophy. It's a big glass bong that's actually bigger than my Emmy."

—Mary-Louise Parker

"It's like Palm Springs without the riffraff."

—Robert Mitchum (about his stint on a California prison farm for his marijuana bust)

"If you look at the way he sang and the way he walked and talked, you could make a pretty good case for somebody who was loaded. He said to me one time when he was really mad, ranting and raving about my heavy drinking, he said, 'Oh that fucking booze. It killed your mother. Why don't you just smoke shit?' That was all he said but there were other times when marijuana was mentioned and he'd get a smile on his face. He'd kind of think about it and there'd be that little smile."

—GARY CROSBY, *BING CROSBY: A POCKETFUL OF DREAMS—THE EARLY YEARS, 1903–1940*

"People at Universal thought I was using drugs, and for years I had the reputation of being a doper. If it hadn't been so damaging, that would have been funny, considering that the only time I'd tried marijuana, years before at a party, it had made me nauseated, and I didn't know what a bong was until my kids told me."

—PATTY DUKE, *CALL ME ANNA*

"Back in the 1950s, two of my best friends in Hollywood were Steve McQueen and Sam Peckinpah, simply because they were the only other guys I knew that smoked dope."

—DENNIS HOPPER

"Being honest is part of who I am, or try to be. By the time you get to my age, you realize it's lots simpler to just tell the truth (with) less covering up, and you need a fantastic memory to keep lying successfully."

—JEFF BRIDGES (WHO LIKES A JOINT ONCE IN A WHILE)

"If you know what you're doing, you don't need to act."

—PETER FONDA

"At a certain point, the early '80s I think, I was sittin' in someone's kitchen and a joint was being passed around, and I just didn't take a second hit. And I never really noticed it happened. The feeling just went away. I'm not saying I won't smoke. I have not taken a psychedelic in a long time. I don't think I could handle it. Timothy Leary said, 'When you get the message, hang up the phone.' I always thought the purpose of psychedelics was information, not entertainment."

—DAVID CARRADINE

"Marijuana you can give up, I've given it up for fifteen years now and it never occurs to me to smoke it anymore."

—LARRY HAGMAN, ACTOR

"Of course drugs were fun."

—ANJELICA HUSTON

"Yeah, fuck all these motherfuckers just picking up a blunt, saying 'I smoke weed.' Fuck you."

—REDMAN

"The thing about us is we're honest. If we're asked whether we take drugs, we say yes. I was brought up by my mam not to be a liar."

—NOEL GALLAGHER OF OASIS

"I'm going to do this for Kristen [Stewart]: So? Listen, Kristen's my best friend. I have nothing to say except that she's amazing."

—NIKKI REED (HER RESPONSE ON THE *TWILIGHT* STAR BEING CAUGHT TAKING A HIT)

FINE FUMES: TWILIGHT

It's a favorite strain of outdoor growers and teenage girls from team Edward and team other dude with the tan and the muscles. This beautiful, purple indica will get you on a munchie kick like a pale demon of the night.

"There's been no top authority saying what marijuana does to you. I really don't know that much about it. I tried it once but it didn't do anything to me."

—JOHN WAYNE

CHAPTER 7

REBELLING AGAINST THE MAN

"Sometimes you need something just to go against the grain. It's like the thrill of the chase."
—Shannon Hoon of Blind Melon

So . . . who is "the man"? Anyone that ganja threatens—and his minions, people afraid of change. We finally got Glenn Beck on our side. That was good, but it's only like step 9 of at least 420. Ted Turner has always been with us, but we need more. We need a pope. We need the Dalai Lama. We need Ellen and Oprah. We need to come out to our families.

As likely as it seems that within a generation or two views about weed in the United States and maybe even the world will change on their own, you can still choose to actively help the cause. Maybe these folks can inspire you. Just don't do anything too crazeballs.

"I'm flattered to be thought of so highly by the U.S. Justice Department that they would use such hyperbole and describe me as a villain."

—MARC EMERY, "PRINCE OF POT"

"All traditional values seemed to be jettisoned by the act of lighting up a joint."

—TIMMEN L. CERMAK, MD, MARIJUANA: WHAT'S A PARENT TO BELIEVE?

"Smoking herb is freedom. If you want to be free, smoke herb."

—BOB MARLEY

"As long as the government keep herb from the people, the people going to keep herb from the government."

—BOB MARLEY

"We need to have a lot of pot, and we need to have millions of millions of people growing this pot. And we need to be able to make the governments waste lots of money tracking all this pot down, so that no matter how much pot they burn, there's still lots of pot."

—MARC EMERY

"We're not going to find someone running for president who advocates reform of those laws. What is required is a genuine republican groundswell."

—WILLIAM F. BUCKLEY, JR.

"Making these arguments in the public square will ultimately do more good than rolling the dice before the Supreme Court."

—RICHARD BROOKHISER, JOURNALIST

"Truth is like marijuana, my boy. A drug on the market."

—ROBERT SHEA AND ROBERT ANTON WILSON, *THE ILLUMINATUS! TRILOGY*

"It's my mission in life to ensure that nobody who is a peaceful, honest, nonviolent cannabis user or grower goes to prison."

—JODIE EMERY

"I use it. I've got post-polio syndrome and it's very helpful. I'm using it until they come and take it away from me."

—ROBERT ANTON WILSON

"Why do so many people invest so much emotion into asking permission of this wretched government—this totally senseless evil fucking regime we live under? '*Please* can we smoke pot?'"

—PETER LAMBORN WILSON

"You know, it was a very different time. There was a war going on. Everything was just a lot more fun."

—ROSEANNE ON *ROSEANNE*

"There is absolutely no greater high than challenging the power structure as a nobody, giving it your all, and winning. . . . No government, no FBI, no judge, no jailer is ever gonna make me say, 'Uncle.'"

—ABBIE HOFFMAN

"Hippy is an establishment label for a profound, invisible, underground, evolutionary process. For every visible hippy, barefoot, beflowered, beaded, there are a thousand invisible members of the turned-on underground. Persons whose lives are tuned in to their inner vision, who are dropping out of the TV comedy of American Life."

—TIMOTHY LEARY, *THE POLITICS OF ECSTASY*

"The spirit of resistance to government is so valuable on certain occasions that I wish it to be always kept alive. It will often be exercised when wrong, but better so than not to be exercised at all. I like a little rebellion now and then. It is like a storm in the atmosphere."

—THOMAS JEFFERSON (TO ABIGAIL ADAMS)

"It's a great sport, base-ball. You can spend eight months on grass and not get busted."

—BOB HOPE (TO THE TROOPS)

"We need the far-out visionary as well as the up-tight academic council which sits in learned judgment on Socrates, Galileo, Bacon, Columbus, Thoreau."

—TIMOTHY LEARY,
THE POLITICS OF ECSTASY

"Between Mitchum and Bur-roughs & Marlon Brando & James Dean & Jack Kerouac, I got myself a serious running start before I was 20 years old, and there was no turning back."

—HUNTER S. THOMPSON, KING-
DOM OF FEAR

"Let's go smoke a joint, man, on the fifty-fuckin'-yard line."

—RORY COCHRANE AS SLATER,
DAZED AND CONFUSED

POT SPOTS: THE FIFTY-FUCKIN'-YARD LINE

This one is risky, but if you want to rebel and stick it to your current or former high school while re-creating a scene from classic stoner cinema, grab your blunts and head out to the football field. There is no more ostentatious place to light up as far as your townies are concerned.

"Richard Nixon called me—I'm proud of this, Space Ghost—he called me the 'most dangerous man alive,' and of course, I tried to be as dangerous to him as I could be."

—TIMOTHY LEARY ON *SPACE GHOST COAST TO COAST*

"I say slack off, because you're only gonna be alive for seventy years, if you're lucky, right? And we just contribute to this sick materialistic society, so slack off, big deal, you know? Have fun. Smoke pot, drink beer, booze, inhale."

—KRIST NOVOSELIC OF NIRVANA

POT SPOTS: SEATTLE

It's not surprising that the birthplace of so many garage grunge bands, like Nirvana, would make for primo bud grounds. There are only like four things you can do in garages: park a car, start a band . . . give up on your band, smoke a bowl. A good time of year to partake in the Emerald City—I shit you not, that's what it's called—is during its annual Hempfest.

"You are more likely to find the evolutionary agents close to jail than to the professor's chair."

—TIMOTHY LEARY, *THE POLITICS OF ECSTASY*

"What kind of hippie am I? Man, I'm a business hippie. I understand the concept of supply and demand."

—DOV TIEFENBACH AS THE HIPPIE STUDENT IN *HAROLD AND KUMAR GO TO WHITE CASTLE*

"Most of the people I run into are interested in being warriors. When they read Tim Leary, or when they go to see a movie by, let's say, Gus Van Sant, or when they go to a Dead concert, they're doing it not just to be entertained; they're doing it because they want to become better warriors. And we've had a real crackerjack bunch of warriors."

—KEN KESEY

"All you kiddies remember to lay off the needle drugs, the only dope worth shooting is Richard Nixon."

—ABBIE HOFFMAN

Todd (Angelo Spizzirri): Dude! When did you get all Haight-Ashbury on me? I mean—you used to listen to Nitzer-Ebb!

Cliff (Ari Gold): I was twelve, and I was a Nazi.

—*GROOVE*

"The Haight is just a place; the Sixties was a spirit."

—KEN KESEY

"Smoking dope and hanging up Che's picture is no more a commitment than drinking milk and collecting postage stamps."

—ABBIE HOFFMAN,
STEAL THIS BOOK

"People today are still living off the table scraps of the sixties. They are still being passed around—the music and the ideas."

—BOB DYLAN

"The '60s are gone, dope will never be as cheap, sex never as free, and the rock and roll never as great."

—ABBIE HOFFMAN

"I don't have an agenda. I smoke pot occasionally, but it's not a big part of my life. I'm not here because I like pot. I'm here because I like freedom."

—ADAM CAROLLA

"What makes us so dangerous is that we're harmless."

—TOMMY CHONG

"They're always going about 'Don't do it,' and 'Say no,' and all that. And you know, that . . . it's just full of shit, innit? Because, you know, I mean, I don't do, you know, smack or crack, or anything rhyming with 'ack,' or, you know, any of the heavy shit. You know, I do all the rest."

—STEPHEN FRY AS A STONER
CHARACTER, *A BIT OF FRY AND
LAURIE*

"Like a lot of old men say, 'Times ain't like they used to be.' I say 'I'm damn glad of it.'"

—MOMS MABLEY

"Was the stuff really that strong, or was it just that our straight, young, virgin middle-class Eisenhower-era minds were so susceptible, so ready to be blown by it?"

—WAVY GRAVY, PEACE ACTIVIST AND WOODSTOCK EMCEE, *CAN'T FIND MY WAY HOME*

"Our country, which we all love so dearly, loves a fucking war, even if it's a war fought in our own streets against our own people."

—PENN JILLETTE, *BULLSHIT!*

"The only way to know the law is to test the law."

—WOODY HARRELSON

"We were telling people at our shows to smoke reefer, to burn their bras, to fuck in the streets."

—WAYNE KRAMER OF MC5, *PLEASE KILL ME: THE UNCENSORED ORAL HISTORY OF PUNK*

"Drugs are to me what the machine gun is to the communists and guerillas."

—PAULO COELHO, *PAULO COELHO: A WARRIOR'S LIFE*

"They are going to write me a letter telling me off; I might burn up a fat one with the letter."

—JON MCCLURE, REVEREND AND THE MAKERS FRONT MAN

"How did they decriminalize marijuana in Massachusetts? They came here [to the Boston Freedom Rally] every year for twenty-odd years. They showed them that they aren't gonna take shit."

—RICK CUSICK, *HIGH TIMES* ASSOCIATE PUBLISHER

POT SPOTS: BOSTON

Boston might not be a stoner paradise. Often there, you'll have no idea what you're smoking, but you just gotta hope for the best. However, this spunky underdog is riding a rebellious streak (for the first time in like two centuries). Since Massachusetts decriminalized the wonder weed, the state has issued many C-note fines—and almost no one has paid them! It's delightful chaos, so visit Boston, learn some history, smoke up, and forget it.

"The worse I do in school, the more I rebel. I drink, I smoke pot, I act like an ass."

—ANDRE AGASSI, *OPEN: AN AUTOBIOGRAPHY*

"I've been the poster boy for the marijuana legalization movement, and it's not fair to those people that actually do it. I've never been involved in that struggle. All I did was speak my mind."

—WOODY HARRELSON

"If this is the way it goes, we'll go underground again. There will be a lot more crime."

—BARRY KRAMER, OPERATOR OF THE CALIFORNIA PATIENT ALLIANCE (RESPONDING TO AN INTOLERANCE OF OVER-THE-COUNTER SALES)

"The more people smoke herb, the more Babylon fall."

—BOB MARLEY (OR SO THE SOUVENIR JAMAICA T-SHIRTS TELL US)

"The war on drugs is a war against marijuana, and the war against marijuana is a war against young people."

—RICK CUSICK, *HIGH TIMES* ASSOCIATE PUBLISHER

"Marijuana is a long-awaited step toward being a grownup and telling society that they can take some part of its anatomy and shove it up another."

—BRIAN GRIFFIN, *THE TRUSTA-FARIAN HANDBOOK*

"History is merely a list of surprises. It can only prepare us to be surprised yet again."

—KURT VONNEGUT

"In fact I think we've reached a point now where the powers that be really have sort of a vested interest in all of us being stoned out as much as possible all the time so we don't know what's going on, and we don't care."

—LESTER BANGS, JOURNALIST AND MUSICIAN

"When I was an art student in the early '60s before the acid scene began I was smoking pot just like anyone else who was an artist."

—BILL GRIFFITH

"Whenever the people are for gay marriage or medical marijuana or assisted suicide, suddenly the 'will of the people' goes out the window."

—BILL MAHER

"I'm a risk taker! I'm growin' an entire crop of marijuana plants in my parents' back yard!"

—ROBERT MUSGRAVE AS BOB IN *BOTTLE ROCKET*

"To marijuana!"

—JESSE L. MARTIN AS COLLINS IN *RENT*

"I have a feeling we smoked pot as much for the high as for the fact it was taboo, and pot was certainly a very good taboo."

—LEWIS BLACK, *NOTHING'S SACRED*

Chong (Tommy Chong): You know what we should invest in? An old age home for hippies . . .

Cheech (Cheech Marin): Oh yeah, we could call it 'Laidback Manor.'

—*NICE DREAMS*

"Don't compromise yourself, honey. You're all you've got."

—JANIS JOPLIN

"The White House drug czar can't stop us any more than he can make water flow uphill."

—ROB KAMPIA, COFOUNDER AND EXECUTIVE DIRECTOR OF THE MARIJUANA POLICY PROJECT

"Politics in the United States consists of the struggle between those whose change has been arrested by success or failure, on one side, and those who are still engaged in changing themselves, on the other."

—HAROLD ROSENBERG, WRITER AND PHILOSOPHER

Andy Botwin (Justin Kirk): How can you be so blindly pro-Bush?

Doug Wilson (Kevin Nealon): I like his wife, Laura. . . . I used to buy weed from her at SMU.

—*WEEDS*

"It would be a terrible time to be in jail in your twenties, because those are such formative years. But by now my philosophy is set. I have a wide circle of people who love me, who care for me. So I didn't ever suffer what I saw others suffer in general."

—MARC EMERY

"There are many other seed sellers, but not ones as mouthy as I am."

—Marc Emery

"There's so much talk about the drug generation and songs about drugs. That's stupid. They aren't songs about drugs; they're about life."

—Cass Elliot

"I've never had a problem with drugs. I've had problems with the police."

—Keith Richards

Chapter 8

Legally Blissed

"If somebody's gonna smoke a joint in their house and not do anybody any harm, then perhaps there are other things our cops should be looking at."

—Sarah Palin

When it comes to getting stoned, the biggest bummer has always been "the man" (and how cops can *always* tell when you're high). In a perfect half-baked world—say, Amsterdam in the 1970s—you could toke out anywhere, anytime, anyhow. But if you're in FloriDUH (or South Carolina or Nebraska or most everywhere else in America), harsh pot laws blunt the joy of blunt—and you could find your ass in jail for way longer than it takes to grow your own. Still, that's no reason not to fight the good fight. The next time you find yourself high among ignorant nonsmokers in, say, Louisiana, toss off a few of these one-liners to prove that while some stoners may drool, pot still rules.

"I have nothing against legalizing it. I hate when they say it's a way to raise revenue for the state. If you want to raise revenue, build something, make something you can sell to China, make a product. It's like Ancient Rome. It's like bread and circuses. It's liquor. It's gambling. It's all sin tax."

—JAY LENO

"It is beyond my comprehension that any humane person would withhold such a beneficial substance from people in such great need simply because others use it for different purposes."

—STEPHEN JAY GOULD, BIOLOGIST AND PALEONTOLOGIST

"It's a joke. Greed and the desire to take drugs are two separate things. If you want to separate the two, the thing you do is make drugs legal. Accept the reality that people do want to change their consciousness, and make an effort to make safer, healthier drugs."

—JERRY GARCIA

"If I were going to legalize a drug, it sure wouldn't have been alcohol. Sorry, there's better drugs and better drugs for you."

—BILL HICKS

"Not only do I think marijuana should be legalized, I think it should be mandatory."

—BILL HICKS

"I don't know why marijuana is still illegal. It has never killed one single individual in all the time we've known about it, yet tobacco kills 300,000 each year, alcohol kills 250,000 each year and they are legal. The laws, the whole thing has been the right wing trying to get back at the civil rights movement: 'What can we do to reverse it? If we can put them in the fucking buses we would, but we can't do that.' As far as I'm concerned, that's all I see."

—GARRETT MORRIS, *LIVE FROM NEW YORK: AN UNCENSORED HISTORY OF SATURDAY NIGHT LIVE*

"People should be more worried about the food habits of Americans, which are probably the worst in the world."

—TOMMY CHONG

"The ill effects of marijuana have been grossly exaggerated in the U.S. Our national drug is alcohol. We tend to regard the use of any other drug with special horror."

—WILLIAM S. BURROUGHS,
NAKED LUNCH

"I do think marijuana should be legalized, though, only for medicinal purposes . . . and recreational."

—KEVIN NEALON

"My point of view, while extremely cogent, is unpopular. . . . That the repressive nature of the legalities vis-à-vis drugs is destroying the legal system and corrupting the police system."

—JACK NICHOLSON

"The minister and anyone else who advocates continued prohibition of cannabis is supporting organized crime. They're supporting the continuation of shootings and murders all across the world related to drug prohibition. My husband tried for a decade to end that death and that suffering with his seed selling so he could fund the movement, fund peaceful democratic change . . . and he never hurt anyone."

—JODIE EMERY

POT SPOTS: VANCOUVER

B.C. Bud! Even though Uncle Sam seems to be rubbing off on Johnny Canuck, the pot culture based in the Couv (as we should all start calling it) is unparalleled in the Western Hemisphere. The Cannabis Culture Headquarters is a must-toke, for high-minded folks above the forty-ninth parallel.

"Herb so good for everything. Why—these people who want to do so much good for everyone who call themselves government and this and that—why them say you must not use the herb?"

—Bob Marley

"Cannabis users and growers are not dangerous unless they're involved with gangs. And gangs are only involved with cannabis growing because of prohibition."

—Jodie Emery

"Marijuana will be legal someday because every law student I know smokes it."

—Lenny Bruce (Larry King loves to use this quote.)

"Aspirin is perfectly legal, but if you take thirteen of them mother-fuckers it'll be your last headache. Long as you been living you ain't never heard a motherfucker overdose on marijuana. You might've thought that n*gga was dead—he ain't dead. He gonna wake up in thirty minutes, hungry enough to eat up everything in your house."

—Katt Williams

"It seems to me now that they know damned well that medical marijuana will have to be accepted eventually. They are trying to stall it until they get a medical product that can be monopolized, that you can't grow in your backyard, a cannabis derivative that can be put out by a large pharmaceutical company."

—ROBERT ANTON WILSON

"The anti-marijuana campaign is a cancerous tissue of lies, undermining law enforcement, aggravating the drug problem, depriving the sick of needed help and suckering well-intentioned conservatives and countless frightened parents."

—WILLIAM F. BUCKLEY JR.

"I don't really believe in legalization under present circumstances because I think that we would find ourselves in a situation where Monsanto would soon own the patent on the DNA of *Cannabis sativa* and *Cannabis indica*. They'll do to marijuana what the conquistadors did to tobacco, which was to turn tobacco from a shamanic drug into an addictive quantity."

—PETER LAMBORN WILSON

"They're willing to kill us to increase their profits."

—ROBERT ANTON WILSON

"Why should we let a couple of jerks who abuse marijuana confuse us about our broader need to help people?"

—DR. OZ

"Well, marijuana is the safest party drug in the world. You cannot die from marijuana. Two thousand college students die every year from alcohol, yet we will not allow them to legally do marijuana. That means two thousand families are devastated this Christmas and every Christmas. It's unbelievable."

—STEPHEN FRY

POT SPOTS: BANGLADESH

If you like your herb legal but still want some risk, Bangladesh may be your stoner oasis. It looks beautiful, has ancient ruins, and is one of the two countries straddled by the largest mangrove forest in the world. *And* it doesn't have any laws prohibiting marijuana. The only issue is safety. From the little info available, it seems to be like a clothes dryer: You put a number of socks (or reporters) in, and some of them just disappear . . . and it gets hot.

"Penalties against possession of a drug should not be more damaging to an individual than the use of the drug itself; and where they are, they should be changed."

—JIMMY CARTER

"I consider marijuana laws to be unjust laws."

—TIMOTHY LEARY

"A method of removing the difficulty of preparing hemp occurred to me. . . . Something of this kind has been so long wanted by the cultivators of hemp, that as soon as I can speak of its effect with certainty I shall probably describe it anonymously in the public papers, in order to forestall the prevention of its use by some interloping patentee."

—THOMAS JEFFERSON

"I'm not afraid of a gang of red-eyed, cotton-mouthed, paranoid stoners coming to jack me for my Visine and cookie dough."

—MARGARET CHO

"I am perswaded, that in many parts of America, your Soil and Climate, is as well calculated for hemp, as that of the Ukraine, and you will not probably think it a difficult matter, to supply Great Britain with that Article."

—SIR JOHN SINCLAIR (1793, TRYING TO SCORE FOR GREAT BRITAIN, IN A LETTER TO ENOCH EDWARDS, PHYSICIAN OF GEORGE WASHINGTON AND BUDDY OF THOM. JEFFERSON)

"Like a lot of other people, I've smoked marijuana. It is what goes on in this country. At the time [the early 1970s], I thought it was a mind-expanding experience, just like a lot of kids and a lot of adults do. Most people who smoke marijuana do it in a way similar to having cocktails in the evening."

—GARY JOHNSON, FORMER GOVERNOR OF NEW MEXICO

"On Monday, the Supreme Court ruled against the use of medical marijuana. Of course, this came as a big shock to marijuana advocates, who showed up to argue the case—today."

—JAY LENO, THE TONIGHT SHOW WITH JAY LENO

"It doesn't seem like an adult twisting up a fatty to watch Nick at Nite is doing any harm, but that's a slippery slope to your kids blowing people behind dumpsters to make money for their heroin habit."

—BILL MAHER

"New York needs to act now to make marijuana legally available for medical use. Every day that we delay is another day of needless suffering for patients like me across the state."

—MONTEL WILLIAMS

"It was pot, in fact, that led me to smoking tobacco."

—DAVID SEDARIS, WHEN YOU ARE ENGULFED IN FLAMES

"I thought this morning, I sat in my office, and I thought, you know what, I think it's about time we legalize marijuana."

—GLENN BECK

"A hammer in the hands of a carpenter can build you a house, but a hammer in the hands of a psychopath will open your skull."

—KEVIN SMITH, SMODCAST

"I felt at no time whenever I ran across some of that good shit, that I was breaking the law, or some foolish thought similar to it."

—LOUIS ARMSTRONG

"Why is it that death by a drug is not the number one reason why it gets to be made illegal?"

—GARRETT MORRIS

"I think it's illogical and irresponsible for you to sentence me to prison because, when you think about it, what did I really do? I crossed an imaginary line with a bunch of plants."

—JOHNNY DEPP AS GEORGE, BLOW

"Back in the early 1970s, we thought we were gonna have marijuana laws decriminalized. We thought it was going to be over. I don't know what happened in between. With many matters of social progress, it's two steps forward, then one step back."

—HUGH HEFNER

"I believe in the right to sovereignty over one's own mind and body."

—STING

"Why would anyone prescribe drugs to treat an illness?"

—STEPHEN COLBERT,
THE COLBERT REPORT

"I'd rather be in a room full of weed smoke than cigarette smoke. With weed smoke I'm looking for a bag of chips, not for a lump in my breast."

—WANDA SYKES, *YEAH,
I SAID IT*

"The problem is that current policies are based on prejudices and fears and not on results."

—CÉSAR GAVIRIA, FORMER
COLOMBIAN PRESIDENT

"While the use of illegal drugs has everywhere skyrocketed over the past 40 years, regardless of the violent persecution of the users of these drugs, the use of tobacco, in a climate of free choice and reliable information, has plummeted to an all-time low."

—RUSS KICK, *YOU ARE STILL
BEING LIED TO*

"In England they always try out new mobile phones in the Isle of Man. They've got a captive society. So I said, you should try the legalization of all drugs on the Isle of Man and see what happens."

—MICK JAGGER

HIGH CREDENTIALS: MICK JAGGER

The 140-pound rock icon and knight has been on the receiving end of some harsh vibes for his recent Rolling Stones documentary. In it, in addition to the use of various less-than-legal substances, there is also an eight-year-old lad whose job it is to roll a joint whenever anyone needs one—obviously the best Take Your Kid to Work Day experience ever. Jagger's idea for isolated experimentation with legalization proves his absolute genius. He uses the very same peer-pressure logic people use to get you to try weed in the first place. Just try it, once. If you don't like it, fine. But just try it. Once. Try it. And if his Isle of Man experiments go poorly, well then we've just got the best cage match ever!

Fellow Stoned Roller, Keith Richards has this to say:

"I smoke weed all the time . . . and can't even remember what happened yesterday."

"Man, if we start arresting everyone for being miserable due to a bad decision, we'd need to cuff everyone who chose to see a Pauly Shore movie."

—PENN JILLETTE, *BULLSHIT!*

"Racial prejudice also helps explain the origins of marijuana prohibition. When California and other U.S. states first decided (between 1915 and 1933) to criminalize marijuana, the principal motivations were not grounded in science or public health but rather in prejudice and discrimination against immigrants from Mexico who reputedly smoked the 'killer weed.'"

—GEORGE SOROS, BILLIONAIRE FINANCIER

"This isn't about getting high. It's about doing what's right."

—TEDDY DUPAY, FORMER COLLEGE BALER

"I don't want to look like a criminal to my children anymore."

—MELISSA ETHERIDGE

"It's time we start dealing with the drug issue as adults, instead of just grouping everything together and hoping it will go away. Grow up and recognize that marijuana is used by huge elements of our population very safely, much to their benefit, in a lot of cases medically, and certainly in their personal lives. I cannot sit by as a nonuser . . . and allow my tax dollars [to be] used to torment a group of people."

—HAL SPARKS

"My closest friend is Jerry Lewis, who has a multitude of back, lung, and various problems. . . . Among the things he was prescribed was Marinol . . . and that's one of the few things that relieves his pain. And I can assure you that to give that medication to someone who is creative and helps other people is also enough reason to use it."

—RICHARD BELZER

"Legalization is a very strong word and has lots of difficult connotations, but the depenalization of marijuana, for example, is a more viable path to begin with."

—JUANES, COLOMBIAN SINGER

"I spent twenty-seven years with Bob Randall, and twenty-five of those years he was using ten marijuana cigarettes a day, federally supplied. And I can assure you he was not a stoner."

—ALICE O'LEARY, *IN POT WE TRUST* (O'LEARY IS THE WIDOW OF ROBERT RANDALL, AN AMERICAN WHO WAS LEGALLY ALLOWED MEDICAL MARIJUANA IN 1988.)

"War is lucrative, including the war on noncorporate drugs. Do I think [marijuana will be legalized within my lifetime]? Probably not."

—WOODY HARRELSON

"It's something that needs to be discussed a little more. It's an economic issue and a violence issue."

—MICHAEL DOUGLAS

"There was one question that was voted on that ranked fairly high, and that was whether legalizing marijuana would improve the economy and job creation. The answer is no. I don't think that's a good strategy to grow our economy."

—BARACK OBAMA (NOTICE "HIGH" AND "GROW." HOPEFULLY, THAT'S CODE FOR "I GOT YOUR BACKS.")

"Here's the point—you're looking at affirmative action, and you're looking at marijuana. You legalize marijuana, no need for quotas, because really, who's gonna wanna work?"

—JON STEWART

"Let us not say that we will decide on a political basis at the national level that no state is competent to regulate the practice of medicine in that state if they decide to allow a doctor to prescribe marijuana, because that is what we are talking about."

—BARNEY FRANK

"The only dead bodies from marijuana are in the prisons and at the hands of the police. This is ridiculous."

—JACK HERER

> **"I view NORML as a small and shrinking dinosaur. NORML's time has come and gone."**
>
> —ROB KAMPIA, COFOUNDER AND EXECUTIVE DIRECTOR OF THE MARIJUANA POLICY PROJECT

"It boils down to 'Old fucks vote.' And that's the problem with this country. Old fucks vote and we don't. We have shit to do. . . . They don't have to work at UPS on Super Tuesday. They have nothing to do—hang around the polls and judge you. . . . [Pro-legalization people] have to put the argument in old people context."

—DOUG STANHOPE

"People can grow pot for them-selves and it's free and whatever, so people aren't going to make a bunch of money off people grow-ing pot to feel better, so they make them rely on pharmaceutical drugs like Marinol that they have to buy from a big company."

—MARK HOPPUS, BLINK 182

FINE FUMES: SPICE AND K2

Victimless criminals and cool law school profs are always on the lookout for the next great legal loophole. A solid idea was syn-thetic cannabis (Spice and K2 the brand names). Sweet, right? Well it hasn't been tested much on humans, and some users report nausea and nasty trips. But it's gotta be safe. Who would ever allow something more dangerous than pot to be legal?

"All drugs of any interest to any moderately intelligent person in America are now illegal."

—Thomas Szasz, psychiatrist

"I know why we can't have a frank discussion with our policy-makers. If you're in the government or in law enforcement you cannot acknowledge that drugs are anything but inherently evil and morally wrong."

—Steven Soderbergh

"We go on a lot in this country about offences being caused by drugs. The truth is just as many offences are caused by drink. And that should be taken into account."

—Jeffrey Archer, author and former British politician

"The prestige of government has undoubtedly been lowered considerably by the prohibition law. For nothing is more destructive of respect for the government and the law of the land than passing laws which cannot be enforced. It is an open secret that the dangerous increase of crime in this country is closely connected with this."

—Albert Einstein

"Three guys were smoking a joint. We said, 'Vote yes on Prop 19,' and they said, 'We're voting no. We're growers.' And we encountered quite a bit of that, a lot of fear about losing their profits. And really I find that despicable that they would rather see people continue to go to prison just to ensure that their pockets keep getting lined."

—Jodie Emery

"What with all the leftover Halloween candy to eat, this is a bad week to try to get stoners to leave the house. If they put a new *Call of Duty* game in the voting booth, this thing would pass, no problem."

—Jimmy Kimmel on *Jimmy Kimmel Live*

"We are on the verge of a historical legislative breakthrough with Proposition 19. It is not a perfect proposition, but it is a huge progressive step towards commonsense drug laws."

—Brad X from Kottonmouth Kings

"More than any other initiative out there, Prop 19 will stabilize our national security and bolster our state economy. It will alleviate unnecessary overcrowding of nonviolent offenders in our state jails, which in turn will help California residents."

—DUSTIN MOSKOVITZ, FACE-BOOK COFOUNDER

"What this movement has always needed is a good lobbyist, you know. We need a kickass, take-no-prisoners kind of guy who will get up at 8:30 in the morning for the breakfast meeting, and that never happened 'cause it's a bunch of stoners."

—BILL MAHER

"This Proposition 19 went a little bit too far, I think, and it was written badly."

—ARNOLD SCHWARZENEGGER

CHAPTER 9

THIS IS YOU ON DRUGS

"Is there lava coming out of my head? I think I'm fine, but I can touch colors."

—Topher Grace (first time stoned)

Heh . . . heh . . .

. . . Heh!

Some of the quotes in this book have been inspirational. Some have been cautionary. Some have shined a light of truth into the darkest parts of our souls. (No? Fine.) This section will do none of those things. This one . . . this will . . . it'll show you what sort of bongs people use. . . . No, that was Chapter 2.

See, I'm eating an all-caramel Milky Way bar, right now, and drinking a Diet Dr Pepper. There's a code under the cap, but I'll never go online and whatever. . . .

Hyde (Danny Masterson): I read somewhere that there are these people in India who fast, man. Yeah. And their minds are so advanced they can actually think themselves to death, man.
Kelso (Ashton Kutcher): I hope I'm not doing that right now. My mind's always doing things that I don't even know about.
Eric (Topher Grace): Man, we always think of so many brilliant things down here, but then later, I can't remember any of them. I mean, they're brilliant, man!

—*THAT '70S SHOW*

"I used to like absinthe, which is like marijuana—drink too much and you suddenly realize why Van Gogh cut off his ear."

—JOHNNY DEPP

"I'm as high as the Himalayas. If I were a city in Germany, I'd be HIGHdelberg."

—DAVID HYDE PIERCE AS NILES
ON *FRASIER*

POT SPOTS: HANFPARADE

This is the largest pot pride parade in Europe. Every August in Berlin, demonstrators tackle a metaphorical wall—and pretend they're not stoned through the whole thing. Part solid demonstration, part ballin' celebration, Hanfparade proves above all that there is a single German word for everything.

"What if all of this is a dream, and it's not even our dream? It's that dog's dream. Maybe we're just existing in his mind, and all of the sudden he'll wake up to go drink out of the toilet, and we'll be gone."

—LINDA CARDELLINI AS LINDSAY ON *FREAKS AND GEEKS*

"I see a carnival of colors. I see grays and browns and grays."

—AMY SEDARIS AS JERRI BLANK
ON *STRANGERS WITH CANDY*

"Spark that spleef. I wanna get high!"

—AMY SEDARIS AS JERRI BLANK
ON *STRANGERS WITH CANDY*

"Do you know how popular I am? I am so popular, everybody loves me so much at this school."

—MOLLY RINGWALD AS CLAIRE IN *THE BREAKFAST CLUB*

"Seriously, no BS: You ever want to rap or anything, just talk or just get weird with somebody, you know, buddies for life."

—BILL MURRAY AS CARL IN *CADDYSHACK*

"Kenneth stared blandly, the kif working. 'You're well aware of my rain obsession,' I said. 'It's always in the rain that the soldier/engineer/apprentice/lorry-driver/master sergeant in the Marines fucks the schoolboy/errand boy/mentally defective farm labourer recently released from Borstal.'"

—JOE ORTON, *THE ORTON DIARIES*

HIGH CREDENTIALS: JOE ORTON

This short-lived and gifted English playwright, known for his dark comedies, chilled with the Beatles and loved his hashish. If you're stoned and feel like a roller coaster of a literary ride, pick up a copy of his diaries. Beautiful descriptions of hash and highs quickly shift to those of aggressive sex with pubescent boys. And you're just like, "This is not going to happen—Oh god, it's happening. Must avert . . . can't . . ." but you are trapped. If you're not comfortable with that mindfuck and just want some good theater, read or see one of his plays.

"I guess you guys are too busy to be bothered by things like mosquito bites. I hear you go in for gardening. The commanding officer says you grow your own grass. . . . In one barracks I passed, a group of GIs was watching 'Twelve O'clock High' and they didn't even have a TV set."

—BOB HOPE TO THE TROOPS,
BOB HOPE: A TRIBUTE

Reporter: You once said you had a drug problem. . . .

Lily Tomlin: Yeah, I still do. It's so hard to find good grass these days.

—MODERN SCREAM

"I just got pulled over. OK, just act cool. You are not drunk. Just a little stoned. 'My license? Uh, isn't it on the bumper?'"

—TOMMY CHONG, CHEECH AND
CHONG: THE UNAUTHORIZED
AUTOBIOGRAPHY

"Is marijuana addictive? Yes, in the sense that most of the really pleasant things in life are worth endlessly repeating."

—RICHARD NEVILLE, PLAY
POWER

"I'll die young but it's like kissing God."

—LENNY BRUCE

"Behind every good man, there's a woman, and that woman was Martha Washington, man, and every day, George would come home, she'd have a big fat bowl waiting for him, man, when he'd come in the door, man. She was a hip, hip, hip lady, man."

—RORY COCHRANE AS SLATER
IN DAZED AND CONFUSED

"Did you ever look at a dollar bill, man? There's some spooky stuff goin' on on a dollar bill, man. I mean, and it's green too!"

—RORY COCHRANE AS SLATER
IN DAZED AND CONFUSED

"I am ridiculously anti-drug. I am so anti-drug that I am above suspicion in any way that involves suspicion, or testing of any kind."

—STEVE CARELL AS MICHAEL
SCOTT ON THE OFFICE

"You know, sometimes I wish I did a little more with my life instead of hangin' out in front of places sellin' weed and shit. Like maybe be an animal doctor. Why not me? I like seals and shit. Or maybe an astronaut."

—JASON MEWES AS JAY IN
CLERKS II

"Daddy's special medicine . . . which you must never use, because it will ruin your life! . . . lets Daddy see and hear magical things that you will never experience. . . . Ever!"

—DAN CASTELLANETA AS
HOMER ON THE SIMPSONS

HIGH CREDENTIALS: JODIE EMERY

The woman behind Marc Emery is Jodie Emery, and while Marc has done so many great things for stoner culture, it seems like Jodie is the Emery to watch. She's one of our most eloquent speakers, with an edgy beauty like a young Shelley Duvall. While Marc awaits release from prison, she is campaigning tirelessly in Canada and abroad for marijuana law reform and running for office. If she broadens her platform beyond just weed (something many of our political hopefuls forget to do), she could actually be the one to change the laws—at least the Canadian ones.

"When the barn burned, we became pawns in marijuana's mellow chess game."

—SETH MACFARLANE AS STAN
ON AMERICAN DAD

"Do you feel lighter, I'm definitely getting lighter. I think I'm becoming immune to gravity."

—SETH MACFARLANE AS ROGER
ON AMERICAN DAD

"I just got a promotion, and it's all thanks to 'Yes I Cannabis.' . . . We have a kitchen?"

—DAN CASTELLANETA AS
HOMER ON THE SIMPSONS

"Oh yeah. This almost makes me not want to stalk that abortion doctor . . . yeah . . . almost."

—UNKNOWN HINSON AS EARLY
CUYLER ON THE SQUIDBILLIES

"I like the camaraderie amongst stoned strippers. It's a certain community that you don't get everywhere else."

—DAVID CROSS

"Do you by any chance poke smot?"

—MERYL STREEP AS JANE IN
IT'S COMPLICATED

Mary Lane (Kristen Bell): Say, is this a fraternity sweater? Is Jimmy hanging out with college boys?

Ralph Wiley (John Kassir): Why, yes, yes, he is. We at Phi Beta . . . Cannabis were so taken with Jimmy, we decided to pledge him . . . early . . . while he's still in high school . . . avoid the rush.

—REEFER MADNESS:
THE MOVIE MUSICAL

"I believe in love. I mean I think that love is very transferable—transformative. I think that love makes things transform."

—JESSE EISENBERG AS JAMES
BRENNAN, ADVENTURELAND

POT SPOTS: AMUSEMENT PARKS
More like "Abusement Park!" Am I right? Am I right? It's widely accepted (not by the parks) that high schoolers are going to experiment here. Each visit becomes a treasure trove of memories. Like, there was always that one midway barker who reeked of pot and always a circumstance that got you banned from a ride. Maybe even ten years later you're still afraid to go on the Viking ship because you're convinced they kept a picture of you in the operator's booth. It's a reasonable concern!

Thomas (David Hemmings): I thought you were supposed to be in Paris.

Verushka (Veruschka von Lehndorff, taking a hit of a joint): I *am* in Paris!

—*BLOW-UP*

"It's cannabis, Sir Herb. It'll tighten your wig."

—LEONARD FREY AS LAU-
RENCE FAGGOT IN *THE MAGIC
CHRISTIAN*

Joe Oramas (Bobby Cannavale): Trains are really cool.

Olivia Harris (Patricia Clarkson): They are.

Finbar McBride (Peter Dinklage): So are horses.

Joe Oramas: What?

Finbar McBride: I was just thinking that.

Joe Oramas: Give me the joint, man.

—*THE STATION AGENT*

"Mmm, pumpkin!"

—GROUCHO MARX AS GOD IN
SKIDOO

"I see a rabbi, and he's performing a circumcision . . . on himself though."

—CHAD EVANS AS A STONER
FRESHMAN IN *VAN WILDER*

"I am not a lump of hash. I'm in charge of Factory Records. I think."

—TONY WILSON, BRITISH
RECORD LABEL OWNER, IN *24
HOUR PARTY PEOPLE*

"Is that really you or am I super stoned?"

—ZACHARY LEVI AS
CHUCK ON *CHUCK*

"I love lasagna. It's so good. And cheesy. You know who else loves lasagna? Garfield. Man, that cat really loves lasagna. Maybe I should put a picture of Garfield in a frame. You know, as a kind of shorthand way of saying 'I love lasagna.' That would be so fucking inside. Or how 'bout a photo of President Garfield? Oh shit, that would be totally meta!"

—ANNA FARIS AS JANE IN
SMILEY FACE

"For shizzle my—that sounds almost Yiddish to me. Yiddish Ebonics."

—SHELLEY BERMAN AS NAT DAVID ON *CURB YOUR ENTHUSIASM*

Eric Montclare (Thomas Lennon): Welcome to your first random drug test!

Pigpen (Derek Hamilton): I don't have to write a test to tell you I do drugs.

—*OUT COLD*

Beverly-Anne (Sue Perkins): Good night, Sir! And happy shagging. Do you think they're on drugs, Beverly-Jane?

Beverly-Jane (Mel Giedroyc): I don't know about them, but I'm buzzing my nut off, Beverly-Anne.

Beverly-Anne: Hmm, me too, Beverly-Jane.

—*GIMME GIMME GIMME*

"That was my skull! I'm so wasted!"

—SEAN PENN AS JEFF SPICOLI IN *FAST TIMES AT RIDGEMONT HIGH*

"Where are those Plaster of Paris paperweights, anyway? I mean that's what I came here to see. . . . That's what I want to see now! Because as we sit here chatting there are important papers flying rampant around my apartment!"

—GRIFFIN DUNNE AS PAUL HACKETT, *AFTER HOURS*

Stan (Trey Parker): Guys, check it out. It's Kenny. Isn't it great? He's just getting high on life.

Kyle (Matt Stone): He's getting *really* high on life.

Cartman (Parker): Dude, he's getting super wasted on life.

—*SOUTH PARK*

Batman (Adam West): Whatever it is, it's . . . it's awfully funny. Ha ha!

Robin (Burt Ward): It's about the funniest trick anyone's ever pulled on us! Ahahaha!

Batman: Funnier than the Joker! I can't . . . I can't stop laughing!

—*BATMAN* (SOME VILLAINS, AS USUAL, OPTING FOR A MYSTERIOUS LAUGHING GAS OVER SIMPLY KILLING THE DYNAMIC DUO)

"Whose hand is that? It's attached to an arm.... Oh! That's my hand."

—STEPHEN COLBERT,
THE COLBERT REPORT

"I'm still stoned. Those eyedrops you gave me didn't do shit."

—KIRSTEN DUNST AS MARY IN
ETERNAL SUNSHINE OF THE
SPOTLESS MIND

"Fortunately, I've been adhering to a pretty strict, uh, drug regimen to keep my mind, you know, limber."

—JEFF BRIDGES AS THE DUDE
IN THE BIG LEBOWSKI

"I wasn't interested in any of the things we talked about. Right now I'm interested in hotcakes."

—SHANNON HOON OF BLIND
MELON

"Oh my God! Look at those dragons!"

—ZACH GALIFIANAKIS (SMOKING
A JAY ON REAL TIME WITH BILL
MAHER)

Jackson Two-Bears (Tom Nardini): Your eyes . . . they're red, bloodshot.
Kid Sheleen (Lee Marvin): You ought to see them from my side.

—CAT BALLOU

"I've got illegals in my bottom."

—CALLUM BLUE AS MASON ON
DEAD LIKE ME

"Don't rescue me yet. I'm getting high as a mother-fucker! Toke, toke, toke, toke! Take it to the head! Take it to the head!"

—Marlon Wayans as Shorty
in Scary Movie 2

"What would it be like to braid Chewbacca?"

—Margaret Cho

"I'm having a little bit of a bad trip. Oh my god! Is that a fucking Liam lookalike or what the hell is that? Is that my boyfriend? Is that my boyfriend?"

—Miley Cyrus (reportedly
on salvia)

FINE FUMES: SALVIA

No, it's not spit. You just flipped the letters. Salvia is a legal herb. Although if its legal status changes, we have Miley Cyrus to blame. In December 2010 she was caught on film taking a salvia hit from a bong—or that's what she claims. Compared to marijuana, there are way less documented salvia trips, but users generally feel disconnected, and they think the people around them look like Picasso portraits.

"Dude, the Atlanteans gave mankind the secret 10,000 years ago to drugs that don't give you a hangover, man. You know what I mean? People are just now starting to use that shit. Embrace it. That's how we're going to solve modern problems. Wisdom of the ancients."

—Ben Affleck as
Dean in Extract

"You know what's

a funny word?

'Pickleweasel.'"

—ASHTON KUTCHER AS KELSO
ON THAT '70S SHOW

"The snozzberries taste like snozzberries."

—GEOFFREY AREND AS A COLLEGE BOY IN SUPER TROOPERS

CHAPTER 10

THIS IS YOUR MOM ON DRUGS

"Just Say No."
—Nancy Reagan and compliant third-graders around the world

Remember in high school, every time your mom yelled at you for smelling like Brad Pitt's pool house, you would think, in your haze, that she could just use a blunt herself? Some of us then may have started aggressively fanning the air around our jackets toward her lungs, to no avail. She only interpreted the spastic movements as "one of those pot fits." And then she'd sit you down for a "rap session." Ugh!

Think about how much easier life would be if the people who yelled at us and preached at us, the ones who claim they love us, just took a chance and tried the thing that we love. Sure you might have to endure the awkwardness of having your dealer and your mom talking about what a great kid you are, but it's worth it. Here are some moms and people of mom disposition who could use a sweet jay from junior.

"Think how loud it would sound if everyone said 'no' at the same time, and that's how loud you should say it when you're offered drugs. So, on the count of three, let's practice saying 'no.' One, two, three. . . . Louder!"

—NANCY REAGAN

"We could have our-selves an old-fashioned ladies' pot party."

—LILY TOMLIN AS VIOLET IN
NINE TO FIVE

Judy (Jane Fonda): Wow! This is . . . this is really good . . . pot. What did you say it was called again?
Violet (Lily Tomlin): Maui Wowie.

—NINE TO FIVE

FINE FUMES: MAUI WOWIE

The Wowie has the distinguished honor of being the credited strain rolled in Cheech and Chong's first shared blunt in *Up in Smoke*. Identifiable as weed by even the most adamant nontokers, this strain has reached mythic proportions. While epic, the name is used so frequently that there's no way to know if you're getting the classic or just a potent Hawaiian herb.

"I just wanted to see what all the hubbub was about. I mean I was skeptical about Tupperware, and that was life changing!"

—DEBRA JO RUPP AS KITTY ON
THAT '70S SHOW

"I'm really starting to worry; there's half-eaten cupcakes everywhere, we're all out of paper clips, and the curtains smell like doob."

—JULIE KAVNER AS MARGE ON
THE SIMPSONS

Maude (Bea Arthur): Go out on the streets. Hang around playgrounds. Jeff, don't come back without the marijuana.

Jeff (Keith Taylor): My luck, I have to have an aunt who's a head.

Maude: Head of what?

—MAUDE (TRYING TO SCORE AS A PROTEST)

"We have to get marijuana out of the movies."

—NANCY REAGAN

"I acted in a youthful and inappropriate way, not in a manner that people have come to expect from me. For this, I am sorry."

—MICHAEL PHELPS (NO WAY! THIS DUDE'S PUBLICIST PROBABLY WROTE THIS ONE.)

"When you're making millions of dollars off of endorsements, you're not just any kid. You're someone who's being paid to be an example. . . . It should have dawned on him by now that every kid wants to be like him. . . . It also kinda begs the question, if he's willing to . . . take a drug that would impede his performance, maybe does it open the door to take a drug that would enhance his performance?"

—ELISABETH HASSELBECK ON
THE VIEW

"Rather than having the courage to stand up and say, 'Look, I just won seven or eight gold medals. Do you think it held me back? How good do you think I would have been if I wouldn't've been smoking pot?' . . . he did the, excuse me, the chicken shit option in this case."

—KEITH STROUP, NORML
FOUNDER

"You look at all these people who graduated from Princeton and Harvard, who are supposed to be pillars of the community. Every day [they're] in the newspaper arrested for some kind of financial fraud. Then you look at someone like Michael Phelps. He's twenty-three. What's he gonna do? He's a kid. He's going to experiment."

—JAY-Z

"We were just celebrating, honestly. It was just a small group, and we were sitting around celebrating."

—MICHAEL PHELPS

HIGH CREDENTIALS: MICHAEL PHELPS

Phelps has dealt with a lot of stress in life: the pressure of winning more gold medals in an Olympics than anyone ever, and the weight of them around his neck must have been killer. But he did it. He did it for America. And all he wanted to do was enjoy a little bong hit . . . but nooooooooo! Sixteen Olympic medals are nothing compared to a puff of pot. He disappointed the anti-pot people, but still had us on his side. Then he disappointed us by apologizing to them! Oh well, here's hoping his millions of dollars in sponsorships help him sleep at night. . . . Yeah, it probably does.

"Thanks Vancouver. You were wonderful. Drive safe. Don't smoke weed! Rock out with your cocks out!"

—BRITNEY SPEARS (AFTER HER SHOW WAS STOPPED FOR THIRTY MINUTES DUE TO MASSIVE AMOUNTS OF WEED SMOKE RUSH-ING THE STAGE IN 2009)

"The bar scene in L.A. is actually horrible because everyone does cocaine and smokes pot and stuff like that. And I hate that shit! I don't like cokeheads and I don't like potheads. And, you know, I smoke pot once in a while. I haven't in a long time, but I like people who drink. I think they're a lot of fun!"

—YELLOW THUNDER WOMAN, SAUSAGE FACTORY: THE COL-LEGE CRIER'S INFAMOUS INTER-VIEWS OF THE FREAKS AND THE FAMOUS

"Personally I think smoking marijuana is very dangerous and it's something I don't do, but I also feel the same way about alcohol, I don't drink that either."

—BERNARD ROSE, FILM DIRECTOR

"Remember this when your courage is tested: you are Americans."

—RONALD REAGAN

"Life can be great, but not when you can't see it. So, open your eyes to life: to see it in the vivid colors that God gave us as a precious gift to His children, to enjoy life to the fullest, and to make it count."

—NANCY REAGAN

"Homosexuality, dope, immorality in general, these are the enemies of strong societies. That's why the Communists and the left-wingers are pushing it. They're trying to destroy us."

—RICHARD NIXON

"Is this why you've never held down a job? Well because, hey, here's something that doesn't take a whole lot of skill to do, just a lighter and a complete lack of self-respect!"

—STEPHEN COLLINS
AS THE DAD ON 7TH HEAVEN

"I see you're smoking pot now! I'm so glad. I think using illegal psychotropic substances is a very positive example to set for our daughter."

—ANNETTE BENING AS CAROLYN
BURNHAM IN AMERICAN BEAUTY

"The only way to catch a doper is when you yourself become a smoker. The surest way to make them bleed is when you bust their ass and steal their weed."

—STACY KEACH AS SGT.
STEDENKO IN NICE DREAMS

Mrs. Fine (Jo Van Fleet): Lose some weight!

Crying hippie (Robert Miller Driscoll): But all I eat is grass and acid.

—*I Love You, Alice B. Toklas!*

"What the hell did you do to my daughter? I swear, if you gave her the weed, I will neuter you!"

—Vincent Ventresca as Dr. Frank Abernathy in *Mammoth*

"You've got the reefer madness!"

—Phyllis Diller as Grandma Titus on *Titus*

"'The Peacocks are not dancing, it will not rain'? Have you smoked ganja?"

—Naseeruddin Shah as Lalit Verma in *Monsoon Wedding*

"You're nothing but a mistake. I should have worn a condom."

—Meat Loaf as Jack's father in *Tenacious D in The Pick of Destiny*

"Hydroponic? I'm not looking for a sound system, my friend. You know what I mean? I'm just looking to get my father a little relief."

—Larry David on *Curb Your Enthusiasm*

"You get a goddamn job before sundown, or we're shipping you off to military school with that goddamn Finkelstein shit kid! Son of a bitch!"

—Strother Martin as Arnold Stoner in *Up in Smoke*

"I don't respond well to mellow, you know what I mean, I have a tendency to . . . if I get too mellow, I ripen and then rot."

—WOODY ALLEN AS ALVY IN
ANNIE HALL

Jack Byrnes (Robert De Niro): If I set you up with the ball, you think you can jump up and spike it?

Greg Focker (Ben Stiller): Yeah, I'd have to be pretty high, but yeah.

Jack: I bet you would, Panama Red.

—MEET THE PARENTS

FINE FUMES: PANAMA RED

There's also a Colombian Red, but you'd never know, because Panama is one of the most well-known strains, referenced often in the media, and it sounds like a badass outlaw. This strain was known for its potency back in the '60s, and while it has competition today, among pot connoisseurs, it's venerated. It's like the Willie Nelson of cultivars.

"I didn't mean it to take on a political tone. I'm just here for the drugs."

—NANCY REAGAN (UNINTEN-
TIONAL HUMOR WHEN TRYING TO
CHANGE THE TOPIC)

"The kids say it makes them think they're going thirty miles an hour when they're going eighty. If that's true, marijuana use should definitely be stopped."

—JOHN WAYNE

"I like life on the natch too much. Besides, it's not possible to make things better when you're spaced out."

—JANE FONDA, MY LIFE SO FAR

"Don't do drugs, because if you do drugs you'll go to prison, and drugs are really expensive in prison."

—JOHN HARDWICK, TV, FILM,
AND THEATER DIRECTOR

"I won't do any dope jokes. I don't like dope jokes. I don't think dope is a joke. That's about the only thing that I would, let's say, resist doing."

—BETTY WHITE

HIGH CREDENTIALS: BETTY WHITE

Okay, these "High Credentials" spaces are reserved for revered stoners, but something needs to be said here. If you've been looking for a way off this Betty White wagon, here it is. She won't do dope jokes. She'll tell you to suck her hypothetical dick (*Lake Placid*) or make you eat her Dusty Muffin (*SNL*), but marijuana is in poor taste? What the hell? Ah shit, I can't be mad at her. I just want Betty White to like what I do.

"Marijuana is a much bigger part of the American addiction problem than most people—teens or adults—realize."

—JOHN WALTERS

"My contention is that marijuana is the most dangerous of all drugs."

—MICHAEL SAVAGE

Here's the problem. Because Amsterdam is so liberal, with drugs specifically, and then you go into the canal zone where the ladies are in the windows...every questionable person in Europe heads to Amsterdam because it's all there in a two-square-mile deal. And their friends are there. It's a Disney World for those people.

—BILL O'REILLY

FINE FUMES: HOLLAND'S HOPE

Well, here is a strain that certain folks could stand to smoke: H.H. is one of the first home team players to light up the Netherlands. Growers like it because it is über mold-resistant. Everyone else likes it because it makes your whole body feel like touching itself. Go Dutch!

"Sometimes I'm asked by kids why I condemn marijuana when I haven't tried it. The greatest obstetricians in the world have never been pregnant."

—ART LINKLETTER

"To me, Doors fans were always the sixteen-year-old idiots at parties, getting stoned, and talking about how Morrison's lyrics were like poetry . . . like that was a deep thought."

—BRUCE MCCULLOCH

"My mother told me when I was very young, She said, 'Son, always keep your bowels open, and nothing can harm you.' And she never said truer words than those."

—LOUIS ARMSTRONG

DePayster (Earl Holliman): You hear about those boys in Nam, smokin' marijuana? Any of my boys do that, I'll kill 'em!
Drake (Darren McGavin): What? What are you talking about, you don't have any "boys."
DePayster: Aw, I'll kill 'em anyway.

—*TRIBES*

"I had always turned it down—to me, smoking pot was absolutely the worst thing in the world. I thought of it as an addiction, and all my friends who smoked it, I felt they really needed help."

—TOMMY RETTIG, FORMER CHILD ACTOR, ADULT SOFTWARE ENGINEER (OR, "SOFTWARE ENGINEER AS AN ADULT"; NOTHING SUGGESTS THE SOFTWARE IS ADULT IN NATURE.)

Celia Hodes (Elizabeth Perkins): I followed Dean here, did you see him?

Nancy Botwin (Mary-Louise Parker): Yes, I did, they were playing poker.

Celia Hodes: Oh, great, now he's going to come home broke, stinking of marijuana. Guess that's better than oriental pussy.

—*WEEDS*

Theodore (Janice Karman): What's that funny smell?

Simon (Ross Bagdasarian): I hate to suggest this, but my guess would be . . . marijuana. An unlawful substance used to experience artificial highs.

—*CARTOON ALL-STARS TO THE RESCUE (THE CHIPMUNKS TEAM UP WITH ALF, SOME LOONEY TOONS, GARFIELD, AND PRESIDENT AND MRS. GEORGE H. W. BUSH TO STOP A TROUBLED TEEN AND AMERICA FROM USING DRUGS.)*

Lamont Sanford (Demond Wilson): The first signs of marijuana use are the hungries, or munchies.

Grady Wilson (Whitman Mayo): Weren't they in *The Wizard of Oz*?

Lamont Sanford: That's Munchkins.

—*SANFORD AND SON*

Hagitha (Tiffani-Amber Thiessen): Who's that? Your grandmother?

Doughy (Tom Arnold): With the bong? Yeah.

Hagitha: Glaucoma?

Doughy: No, spring break.

—*SHRIEK IF YOU KNOW WHAT I DID LAST FRIDAY THE THIRTEENTH*

Joy Burns (Patricia Clarkson): Honey, roll it tighter next time.

Timmy Burns (John Gallagher Jr.): Sorry, mom.

—*PIECES OF APRIL*

For as long as there have been moms, there have been kids trying to figure them out, and for almost as long, the kids have been using weed to gain insight.

"Conservative parents' groups opposed to marijuana had helped to ignite the Reagan Revolution. Marijuana symbolized the weakness and permissiveness of a liberal society; it was held responsible for the slovenly appearance of teenagers and their lack of motivation."

—DAN BAUM, *SMOKE AND MIRRORS*

"I can understand straight people because they operate on fear. They do not want to change jobs because they fear they can't get another one."

—TOMMY CHONG

"Bob, we're just tired of the way you run your interventions."

—DAVID CROSS AS DAVID, *MR. SHOW WITH BOB AND DAVID*

"Them say it might get you mad. But all this is true! 'Cause them never make themselves, they don't know what power, what strength them have . . . and the more they look 'pon the thing, they get afraid of themselves."

—BOB MARLEY, *EVERY LITTLE THING GONNA BE ALRIGHT: THE BOB MARLEY READER*

"I recently read an interview in *Rolling Stone*, where he advocated that people should not do drugs, *Keith Richards* said that we should not do drugs. Keith, we can't do any more drugs, *because you already fuckin' did them all!* There's none left; we have to wait until you die so we can smoke your ashes, alright!"

—DENIS LEARY

"I never smoked marijuana in high school. Never touched it, 'cause Nancy Reagan had this amazing marketing campaign, ok. 'Just Say No.' Get up and look at the cartoons in the morning, there'd be an egg on the TV right, then they'd cut to a frying pan. It's like 'This is your brain. This is your brain on drugs.' And you're like, 'Fuck that! Fuck fuck fuck it.'"

—TOM GREEN

"There's only two kinds of people who are against drugs: the people who've never done drugs and the people who've really sucked at doing drugs."

—DOUG STANHOPE

"Reality is a crutch for people who can't cope with drugs."

—LILY TOMLIN

"Conservatives pride themselves on resisting change, which is as it should be."

—WILLIAM F. BUCKLEY, JR.

"So, yesterday Dwight found half a joint in the parking lot. Which is unfortunate, because, as it turns out, Dwight finding drugs is more dangerous than most people using drugs."

—JOHN KRASINSKI AS JIM ON *THE OFFICE*

"There are now more teens going into treatment for marijuana dependency than for all other drugs combined."

—JOHN WALTERS

Chapter 11

A Natural High

*"Everything I'm wearing right now is made of hemp . . .
including . . . these shoes are hemp too."*
                                        —Woody Harrelson

Stoners are beyond going green: We're green and gone.
Organic living, herbal healing, and guessing what animals
are thinking are all natural extensions of the fact that we
appreciate the Earth and the things that poke out of it.

Nature is powerful. It's what makes most documen-
taries interesting. It's why a self-loathing anyone is self-
loathing. And it's what gave superpowers to all of the
X-Men, who by the way, now live in San Francisco where
teammate Pixie flies around sprinkling hallucinogenic dust
on folks.

Nature is the shit. And most stoners respect that.

"They've outlawed the number one vegetable on the planet."

—TIMOTHY LEARY

"And what is a weed?

A plant whose vir-

tues have not yet

been discovered."

—RALPH WALDO EMERSON

"But they whom truth and wisdom lead, can gather honey from a weed."

—WILLIAM COWPER

"It's nature. I mean, how do you make nature against the fucking law? It grows everywhere, serves a thousand different functions, all of them positive. To make marijuana against the law is like saying God made a mistake."

—BILL HICKS

"I think people need to be educated to the fact that marijuana is not a drug. Marijuana is an herb and a flower. God put it here. If He put it here and He wants it to grow, what gives the government the right to say that God is wrong?"

—WILLIE NELSON

"Marijuana in its natural form is one of the safest therapeutically active substances known to man."

—DEA ADMINISTRATIVE LAW JUDGE FRANCIS L. YOUNG

"It is time we stop driving the American people to drink. Instead, we should simply and logically allow them to use a safer alternative, if that is what they prefer."

—NORM STAMPER, FORMER CHIEF OF THE SEATTLE POLICE DEPARTMENT, *MARIJUANA IS SAFER: SO WHY ARE WE DRIVING PEOPLE TO DRINK?*

"Even when we did drugs we meant well, we said, or at least we meant no harm; if nature was good, then all nature's gifts were good, right?"

—LINDA ELLERBEE, *MOVE ON*

"If your life is fucked up, you need weed. Weed is put on this Earth for n*ggas on the struggle, n*ggas on the grind. There is a chemical in weed that's called 'fuckit.'"

—KATT WILLIAMS

"Growing marijuana

is a natural act. Since

the 1930s, Americans

have been denied the

right to grow this use-

ful, beneficent friend."

—MOUNTAIN GIRL, *PRIMO PLANT: GROWING MARIJUANA OUTDOORS*

HIGH CREDENTIALS: MOUNTAIN GIRL

Aka Carolyn Adams/Garcia, Mountain Girl is a former member of Ken Kesey's Merry Pranksters and a former wife of Jerry Garcia. That cements her hippie and weed cred there, but she is also an authority on the cultivation of cannabis. She even wrote a book about it, *Primo Plant*, to share her expertise with the world.

"Sweetness has proved to be a force in evolution. By encasing their seeds in sugary and nutritious flesh, fruiting plants such as the apple hit on an ingenious way of exploiting the mammalian sweet tooth: in exchange for fructose, the animals provide the seeds with transportation, allowing the plant to expand its range."

—MICHAEL POLLAN, *THE BOTANY OF DESIRE*

FINE FUMES: BUBBLEGUM

If you like your sticky sweet, the strains that go by "Bubblegum" will get your taste buds skanking. Besides the flavor, it's also a lot like chewing gum in that you'll often find it covertly stuck to the undersides of desks and chairs.

"One of the main reasons corn cannot be used—and it's really commonsense knowledge—is that corn only yields one or two ears to the stalk and it grows in eighteen-inch and two-foot rows. . . . This is a reason why we would use hemp. It would grow fence row to fence row yielding no space in between the rows, and be grown like hair on a dog's back, like wheat, like oats."

—CRAIG LEE, CURATOR OF THE KENTUCKY HEMP MUSEUM AND LIBRARY

HIGH CREDENTIALS: TED TURNER

Here is our bankroll. Media mogul Turner, who has been reported to enjoy a quiet joint in his office, is very pro-pot. His Turner Foundation is a major sponsor of the Kentucky Hemp Museum. It's not so surprising, then, that things like *Harvey Birdman: Attorney at Law* and *Space Ghost: Coast to Coast* are birthed into existence on his networks.

"Man, despite his artistic pretensions, his sophistication, and his many accomplishments, owes his existence to a six-inch layer of topsoil and the fact that it rains."

—ANONYMOUS, BUT SO WIDELY QUOTED

"The greatest service which can be rendered any country is to add an useful plant to its culture."

—THOMAS JEFFERSON

"Why ban herb? Him a vegetable, just like spinach. You can cook him and eat him. That's why God put him on the earth."

—BOB MARLEY

"I like to take a toothpick and throw it in the forest and say, 'You're home!'"

—MITCH HEDBERG

"Why is marijuana against the law? It grows naturally upon our planet. Doesn't the idea of making nature against the law seem to you a bit . . . unnatural?"

—BILL HICKS

"Whether they legalize it or not it's not stopping anyone. You know I'm saying? I mean, it's a plant. But, I think, what's most important—than even pot—is hemp. Why? Because pot—yeah, people smoke marijuana, whatever—but hemp can save the planet."

—ZIGGY MARLEY

"Once, I woke up with a spider running across my face, and I thought, 'So a spider is running across my face,' and brushed him off gently, 'it's his world, too.'"

—ROBERT SHEA AND
ROBERT ANTON WILSON,
THE ILLUMINATUS! TRILOGY

"An acre of the best ground for hemp, is to be selected, and sown in hemp and to be kept for a permanent hemp patch."

—THOMAS JEFFERSON

"I grow and sell marijuana. It's organic. It's therapeutic. It's of the earth . . . like tomatoes."

—MARY-LOUISE PARKER AS
NANCY BOTWIN, *WEEDS*

"If you have to sleep, count sheep. Don't count endangered animals; you will run out."

—MITCH HEDBERG

"Seeds are a very hearty life form and strongly desire to grow and flourish. But some of them need people's help to get started. Plant your seeds."

—GREG HILL (MALACLYPSE THE
YOUNGER) AND KERRY THORN-
LEY (OMAR KHAYYAM RAVEN-
HURST), *PRINCIPIA DISCORDIA*

"There is not a sprig of grass that shoots uninteresting to me."

—THOMAS JEFFERSON

"Man, they ain't nothin' wrong with smokin' weed. Weed is from the Earth. God put this here for me—and you! Take advantage, man. Take advantage."

—CHRIS TUCKER AS SMOKEY,
FRIDAY

"I love to think of nature as unlimited broadcasting stations, through which God speaks to us every day, every hour and every moment of our lives, if we will only tune in and remain so."

—GEORGE WASHINGTON CARVER

"I especially enjoy sharing the marijuana. It's a joy to cut a stem of Blueberry marijuana, thick with flower buds and fall color in the leaves, to lie on the table or the bed of a patient."

—CHEMO SABE, *MEDICAL MARI-
JUANA CAREGIVER'S JOURNAL*

"The problem is, nothing's really changed yet and we live in a society where the economy is based on all these giant industries that are raping Mother Earth."

—WOODY HARRELSON

"Marijuana is an awesome herbal remedy for most ailments and should be taken very seriously. Its recreational purposes should not be abused and those committed should clear the space for it, just as you would if you were going to have a five-hour massage or take LSD."

—JASON MRAZ

"It's just land with a couple of jaded barns that need to be renovated. It's a nice place to camp but my long-term plan is to grow industrial hemp for making paper and material. When I stop touring I'm going to hang around there and start shearing sheep."

—MATT BELLAMY OF MUSE

Fashion Designer Tara Lynn: The gown is a simple princess line with an open back; a machine-knit hemp twine strap crisscrosses in back.

Crystal Bowersox: The train of the dress is a handmade design of hemp twine, sea shells, and beads, some of which came from pieces of sentimental jewelry. (discussing the *American Idol* contestant's earth-friendly wedding gown)

"I had heard about Tara Lynn and it was very appealing to go 'green' for Miss America. I will be making a significant statement and suspect I will be the only contestant who has chosen to go this route."

—ASHLEY WHEELER, MISS VERMONT 2008 (ON HER HEMP GOWN)

"Small farms, strong communities, sustainable living. You know, every good value that exists in this county is what we're gonna try to embody in a tourist trap."

—MATT COHEN, GROWER

"A weed is no more than a flower in disguise,
   Which is seen through at once, if love give a man eyes."

—JAMES RUSSELL LOWELL, POET

"I love having my hands in the dirt. It is never a science and always an art. There are no rules. And if it comes down to me versus that weed I'm trying to pull out of the ground that doesn't want to come out? I know I'll win."

—MATTHEW MCCONAUGHEY

"Growing hemp as nature designed it is vital to our urgent need to reduce greenhouse gases and ensure the survival of our planet."

—JACK HERER

"Industrial hemp is a very useful plant. I challenged the attorney general to get rid of the criminal stigma associated with hemp so we can look at it in terms of how it might be useful."

—Jesse Ventura

"The [hemp] fiber itself is the strongest natural fiber in the world."

—Steve Levine, president of Hemp Industries Association in *The Union*

"Bank tellers are fatalistic; clerks are fatalistic. I'm a farmer. Who ever heard of a fatalistic farmer?"

—Bob Dylan

FINE FUMES: *CANNABIS RUDERALIS*

If sativa and indica are the adored son and daughter of the Cannabis family, ruderalis is the kid in the attic. It's a great grower. It just sucks in the THC department. But it does have its uses: It can be used for hemp, and it can also be fancily spliced up with the other species to make strong plants that pack a punch when you pack your bowl.

"Littering and . . . littering and . . . littering and smokin' the reefer."

—Jay Chandrasekhar as Thorny in *Super Troopers* (reasons to pull a dude over)

"It is a peaceful, botanical revolution, overthrowing the government with our slogan. What a great way to have revolution. Nobody gets hurt; everyone grows a lot of plants. Nobody dies."

—Marc Emery

"Of all that Orient lands can vaunt
Of marvels with our own competing,
The strangest is the Haschish plant,
And what will follow on its eating."

—FROM "THE HASCHISH" BY JOHN GREENLEAF WHITTIER

FINE FUMES: HINDU KUSH

Taking its name from some "Orient lands," Hindu (and other Kush strains) comes from the mountains in Afghanistan, though it probably wasn't growing on a snowcap. The word *kush* in Persian means "to kill," which is kind of a buzz kill. "Hindu Koosh" seems more relatable. Either way, it's good for a mellow, all-around high.

Doyle (Stephen Baldwin): Hi, I'm Doyle.

Bud (Pauly Shore): And I'm Bud.

Both: And when we're not saving the environment, we're thinkin' of you, naked, thigh deep in tofu.

—*BIO-DOME*

"This is Henry Hemp. I represent the male energy of the hemp plant: food, fabric, fuel, fiber, because my sister MaryJane is misunderstood."

—HENRY HEMP, UNOFFICIAL MASCOT AND ACTIVIST

"To the artist, there is never anything ugly in nature."

—AUGUSTE RODIN

"To be young, good-looking, healthy, famous, comparatively rich, and happy is surely going against nature."

—JOE ORTON

CHAPTER 12

HIGH ON GOD

"The so-called 'drug culture' was not a campus fad; it was a world-wide revival of the oldest religions going."
—Timothy Leary

People have been smoking up for thousands of years. Seriously, thousands and thousands. Way before the Rastafarians and Bob Marley. (Rest in peace.)

Look through the Bible—grass is everywhere! And what about giraffes and platypuses? Try to tell me weed wasn't involved in their creation. And you know they smoked a little herb every now and again in ancient India. And don't even get me started about the Olympians. God, I love Spartans.

Maybe it was a religious practice, maybe people wanted to find the meaning of life (Is it possible to get higher than high? How high can you go? Higher than the Big Man? Wait, what's higher than high?), or maybe they just had a bad day. Dope helps you with all these things and more.

So relax, man, roll that joint, and find a little spirituality with guidance from fellow followers of the THC ministry.

"He causeth the grass to grow for the cattle, and herb for the service of man: that he may bring forth food out of the earth."

—PSALMS 104:14

"And the earth brought forth grass and herb yielding seed after its kind, and the tree yielding fruit, whose seed was in itself, after his kind: and God saw that it was good."

—GENESIS 1:12

"For so the Lord said to me, I will take my rest, and I will consider in my dwelling place like a clear heat on herbs, and like a cloud of dew in the heat of harvest."

—ISAIAH 18:4

"Not that which goeth into the mouth defileth a man; but that which cometh out of the mouth, this defileth a man."

—MATTHEW 15:11

"And he showed me a river of water of life, clear as crystal, proceeding from the throne of God and of the Lamb. In the midst of the street thereof, and on both sides of the river, was the tree of life, bearing twelve fruits, yielding its fruits every month, and the leaves of the tree were for the healing of the nations."

—REVELATIONS 22:1–2

"If you smoke, smoke herb. Rastaman use herb for meditation. Especially in our busy world like this, you smoke herb . . . what is going on, it still can't trouble you . . . keep your meditation."

—BOB MARLEY, *EVERY LITTLE THING GONNA BE ALRIGHT: THE BOB MARLEY READER*

POT SPOTS: JAMAICA

If you're taking the Rasta route with your ganja, there's really no excuse not to visit Jamaica. Marley's house has been turned into a museum, so you can go chill in his living room/gift shop. Casual pot tourists will have a good time too, though as usual, fun is illegal. Keep the smoking to yourself in the confines of your resort. There will likely be someone waiting at the gates to sell it to you.

"You don't need herb to write a song, but it frees the mind. We still have the word of the Almighty. But herb in any form—food, drink, tea, cake—we love herb. In Jamaica, 95 percent of the people smoke herb. You can't stop that."

—Julian Marley

"What really happened was that everybody was squabbling over the apple and working up a sweat and pushing one another around and pretty soon their vibrations . . . heated up the apple enough to unleash some heavy fumes. In a word, the Olympians all got stoned."

—Robert Shea and Robert Anton Wilson, *The Illuminatus! Trilogy* (their take on the Golden Apple)

"That staying up all night to smoke ganja and dance and sing can be passed off as religious activity was something we learned from the Bauls of Bengal."

—Kerry Thornley, *Principia Discordia* (5th edition introduction)

"And the Angel of Eris bade of the Lord: Go ye hence and lift the Stash, that you may come to own it and, owning it, share it and, sharing it, love in it and, loving in it, dwell in it and, dwelling in the Stash, become a Poet of the World and a Sayer of Sayings—an Inspiration to all men and a Scribe to the Gods."

—Greg Hill (Malaclypse the Younger) and Kerry Thornley (Omar Khayyam Ravenhurst), *Principia Discordia*

"'Tell me you dumb beast,' demanded the Priest in his commanding voice, 'why don't you do something worthwhile. What is your purpose in life, anyway?'

Munching the tasty grass, The Sacred Chao replied 'Mu.'*

Upon hearing this, absolutely nobody was enlightened. Primarily because no one could understand Chinese.

*'Mu' is the Chinese ideogram for NO-THING."

—GREG HILL (MALACLYPSE THE YOUNGER) AND KERRY THORNLEY (OMAR KHAYYAM RAVENHURST), *PRINCIPIA DISCORDIA*

"I do not consider myself a religious person in the usual sense, but there is a religious aspect to some highs. The heightened sensitivity in all areas gives me a feeling of communion with my surroundings, both animate and inanimate."

—CARL SAGAN

"Like the Catholic Church on the issues of birth control, celibacy, and female priests, the federal government's rhetoric on drugs has left it precious little wiggle room."

—DAN SAVAGE, *SKIPPING TOWARDS GOMORRAH*

"God writes the gospel not in the Bible alone, but on trees and flowers and clouds and stars."

—MARTIN LUTHER

"It's a gift from God."

—MICHELLE PHILLIPS

"The voices of St. Francis, Socrates, General Gordon, and Timothy O'Leary all told me I was God."

—PETER O'TOOLE AS THE 14TH EARL OF GURNEY, *THE RULING CLASS*

"Whether drugs lead to illumination or degradation depends on the spirit in which one takes them."

—GEORGE ANDREWS, *DRUGS AND MAGIC*

"Maybe this world is another planet's hell."

—ALDOUS HUXLEY

"The world is ready for a mystic revolution, a discovery of the God in each of us."

—GEORGE HARRISON

"We're living proof that heaven watches out for fools and small children."

—CHEECH MARIN

HIGH CREDENTIALS: MICHELLE PHILLIPS

As the last surviving member of the Mamas and the Papas, Michelle really has control over what the band's legacy will be—unless stepdaughter Mackenzie Phillips saved some material for a second tell-all. Luckily for us, Michelle has decided to speak out for marijuana law reform. She is a member of the Marijuana Policy Project's advisory board—which just seems to be a bunch of celebrities, but still, we're hoping this Mama gets her way and that maybe California dreams really do come true.

HIGH CREDENTIALS: CHEECH MARIN AND TOMMY CHONG

Cheech and Chong are pioneers of stoner comedy and stoner cinema. We've been pegged as slackers ever since their success, but who can hold it against them? The first scene where Cheech and Chong meet in *Up in Smoke* features some of the most entertaining shit (literally, though it's wrapped in a joint) ever filmed.

"Wine's okay because Jesus drank that."

—MARY-KATE OLSEN AS TARA
ON *WEEDS*

Jesus (Robert Torti): Jimmy, take a hit of God instead. You think you can handle the high?
Jimmy (Christian Campbell): I've got a new god now!

—*REEFER MADNESS:
THE MOVIE MUSICAL*

"I think sex is one of the five highest sensations one can experience. A very high orgasm is a way of communication with our Creator."

—PATTI SMITH

"In ancient India, bhang was so sacred that it was reputed to deter evil, bring luck, and cleanse the user of sin. Harm and disaster visited those who trod upon the holy leaves of the hemp plant."

—RICHARD E. SCHULTES, "MAN AND MARIJUANA," *NATURAL HISTORY MAGAZINE*, VOL. 82

"The favorite drink of Indra, god of the firmament, was prepared from Cannabis. The Hindu god Siva taught that the word 'bhangi' must be chanted prayerfully over and over at the time of sowing, weeding, watering, and harvesting the holy plant."

—RICHARD E. SCHULTES, "MAN AND MARIJUANA," *NATURAL HISTORY MAGAZINE*, VOL. 82

"The purpose of the California Cannabis Ministry is to reclaim legitimate spiritual values inherent to agriculture."

—PAUL J. VON HARTMANN, CHURCH MEMBER

"A 29-year-old electrical technician who describes his meditation practice as an eclectic mixture of early Christian and oriental techniques writes: 'I find my ability to center in while stoned is increased. This is also the factor of 'letting go' which is enhanced during meditation. To me getting stoned is a communion of sorts with the God-head.'"

—CHARLES T. TART, PHD, *ON BEING STONED*

"That's right, Mom! I'm smoking weed with the Reverend's son! He works in mysterious ways indeed!"

—YOUTH, IN STEW'S *PASSING STRANGE*

"Just because I'm high doesn't mean that every message coming is the word of God. It can also be that some of the false beliefs are a little louder as well."

—ALANIS MORISSETTE

"I think it needs to have an intention for use; a time and place, for spiritual and healing purposes."

—JASON MRAZ

"My generation, faced as it grew with a choice between religious belief and existential despair, chose marijuana. Now we are in our Cabernet stage."

—PEGGY NOONAN, JOURNALIST

"Do you think God gets stoned? I think so . . . look at the platypus."

—ROBIN WILLIAMS

"Johnny Cash was plenty good enough to fool his fans. They believed he felt it in his soul when he sang the Gospel while stoned on drugs."

—SUZANNE FIELDS, NATIONALLY SYNDICATED COLUMNIST

"Oh yeah, the preacher's kid has to be the baddest one. If everyone is smoking weed, we've got to smoke crack. If you're throwing rocks, we've got to throw bigger rocks."

—NICK CANNON

"If there was no faith there would be no living in this world. We could not even eat hash with any safety."

—HENRY WHEELER SHAW, HUMORIST

"Ganja has everything to do with the upliftment of the mind, to motivate inspiration."

—PETER TOSH

"I felt at one with the universe. I had never felt this before. Delusional or not, it was something I never found at temple and it has been a comfort to me ever since."

—LEWIS BLACK, *NOTHING'S SACRED*

"The use of drugs on its own does not necessarily lead to enlightenment. Any group, ancient or modern, which confuses the use of particular substances with sanctity itself is destined for disillusionment."

—GEORGE ANDREWS, *DRUGS AND MAGIC*

"All that we are is the result of what we have thought."

—BUDDHA

FINE FUMES: BUDDHA CHEESE

The personification of enlightenment combined with Kraft singles? Yes, please! With a cheesy smell like right out of the Cheez-It box (if you ate the crackers and hid your stash in there) Buddha Cheese and other cheese strains have been welcomed with open arms and emptied bowls into the cannabis community.

"I discovered smoking pot—that, plus listening to rock music. And there was peer pressure, so the Jesus thing became really boring, and I don't know that I ever, really believed in all those things."

—KEITH HARING, ARTIST AND ACTIVIST, *KEITH HARING: THE AUTHORIZED BIOGRAPHY*

"A drug is neither moral nor immoral—it's a chemical compound. The compound itself is not a menace to society until a human being treats it as if consumption bestowed a temporary license to act like an asshole."

—FRANK ZAPPA

"Hey, do I preach to you when you're lying stoned in the gutter? Noooo. So beat it!"

—JOHN DI MAGGIO AS BENDER, *FUTURAMA*

"There is not much sense in suffering, since drugs can be given for pain, itching, and other discomforts. The belief has long died that suffering here on earth will be rewarded in heaven. Suffering has lost its meaning."

—ELISABETH KÜBLER-ROSS,
PSYCHIATRIST

"The whole LSD, STP, marijuana, heroin, hashish, prescription cough medicine crowd suffers from the 'Watchtower' itch: you gotta be with us, man, or you're out, you're dead. This pitch is a continual and seeming must with those who use the stuff. It's no wonder they keep getting busted."

—CHARLES BUKOWSKI, POET
AND NOVELIST

"I am a golden God!"

—BILLY CRUDUP AS RUSSELL
HAMMOND IN ALMOST FAMOUS

"I try to worship two or three times a day because you know what? You can never worship God too many times."

—REVEREND BUD GREEN

"If organized religion is the opium of the masses, then disorganized religion is the marijuana of the lunatic fringe."

—KERRY THORNLEY, PRIN-
CIPIA DISCORDIA (5TH EDITION
INTRODUCTION)

Chapter 13

Stoner Utopia

"Good evening everyone. Our top story: Marijuana is now legal . . . leg— . . . is now legal . . . legal . . . in Quahog, and it's made everything . . . just so great."
—Seth MacFarlane as Tom Tucker on *Family Guy*

What if every church bake sale was a church "baked" sale? What if in *Field of Dreams* Kevin Costner hears voices from a weed field saying, "If you build it . . . wait, what?" And what if in *The Lost World: Jurassic Park* the velociraptors chase the dudes through acres of sticky just to say, "Hey, man, let's go play Skee-Ball."

Sure, it's an ideal, but one we get closer to every day. A major benchmark will be widespread acceptance, which many conservatives fear. But what's the worst that could happen? Here are some thoughts on why a worldwide hash bash might not be so bad.

"Look, Lois, ever since marijuana was legalized, crime has gone down, productivity is up, and ratings for *Doctor Who* are through the roof."

—SETH MACFARLANE AS BRIAN
GRIFFIN ON *FAMILY GUY*

"There are a lot of countries where it's perfectly legal, and they get along better than America. Plus it may be our only chance to go to the Playboy Mansion and hang out."

—COURTNEY TAYLOR-TAYLOR OF
THE DANDY WARHOLS

"It's happening and they can slow it down and cause people to be less regulated and not be able to pay taxes, but they're not going to be able to stop it."

—RICHARD LEE, MAYOR OF
OAKSTERDAM

"U.S. statistics of the 1970s indicate that you will live eight to 24 years longer if you substitute daily cannabis use for daily alcohol and tobacco use. New research is outlawed, of course."

—JACK HERER, *THE EMPEROR
WEARS NO CLOTHES*

"The first classes you will be required to take will be Politics and Legal Issues. We have lawyers come in and talk about what the laws are and aren't. Then we move on to cooking, hash making, bud tending. We have 'Cannabusiness' to learn how to start a dispensary or production facility."

—RICHARD LEE, ALSO THE PRES-
IDENT AND FOUNDER OF OAK-
STERDAM UNIVERSITY

POT SPOTS: OAKSTERDAM

Oakland, California, was off the radar for a while after *Hangin' with Mr. Cooper* went off the air, but cut to 2005: California sanctions medical stashes, and we start to bring a little of the Netherlands stateside. With dispensaries, cafes, and even an academic institution, Oaksterdam is a domestic mecca for frequent buyers with frequent fliers. And Mark Curry, contact me ASAP about the stoner reboot of *Coop*!

"It would cut the crime rate in half. All the stoners I know are too paranoid to do anything stupid."

—JUSTIN TIMBERLAKE

"I've never been a major smoker, but I think America's view on weed is ridiculous. I mean—are you kidding me? If everyone smoked weed, the world would be a better place."

—KIRSTEN DUNST

"The fact is that so many people have used marijuana and aren't screaming, slobbering lunatics. Eventually, this generation that has familiarity with marijuana will come to power, at which point [legalization] will just happen."

—STEPHEN EASTON, PROFESSOR OF ECONOMICS FOR SIMON FRASER UNIVERSITY

"Marijuana is like Coors beer. If you could buy the damn stuff at a Georgia filling station, you'd decide you wouldn't want it."

—BILLY CARTER

"If we could sniff or swallow something that would, for five or six hours each day, abolish our solitude as individuals, atone us with our fellows in a glowing exaltation of affection and make life in all its aspects seem not only worth living, but divinely beautiful and significant, and if this heavenly, world-transfiguring drug were of such a kind that we could wake up next morning with a clear head and an undamaged constitution—then, it seems to me, all our problems (and not merely the one small problem of discovering a novel pleasure) would be wholly solved and earth would become paradise."

—ALDOUS HUXLEY

"From my own work and the experiences of other members of the law enforcement community, it is abundantly clear that marijuana is rarely, if ever, the cause of harmfully disruptive or violent behavior."

—NORM STAMPER, FORMER CHIEF OF THE SEATTLE POLICE DEPARTMENT, *MARIJUANA IS SAFER: SO WHY ARE WE DRIVING PEOPLE TO DRINK?*

"Rum teach you to be a drunkard. And herb teach you to be someone."

—BOB MARLEY

"Anyway, no drug, not even alcohol, causes the fundamental ills of society. If we're looking for the source of our troubles, we shouldn't test people for drugs, we should test them for stupidity, ignorance, greed and love of power."

—P. J. O'ROURKE

"I've never met someone who smokes pot and goes home and beats their wife up. I've met a lot of people who drink and do that."

—JESSE VENTURA (SOUNDS LIKE HE HAS A GREAT GROUP OF FRIENDS.)

"I was a heavy drinker, but the alcohol affected my heart rather than my liver. So I stopped. And I miss it. I really like that kind of life. I smoke grass now. I say that to everybody, because marijuana should be legalized. It's ridiculous that it isn't. If at the end of the day I feel like smoking a joint I do it. It changes the perception of what I've been through all day."

—ROBERT ALTMAN

"To punish drug takers is like a drunk striking the bleary face it sees in the mirror. Drugs will not be brought under control until society itself changes, enabling men to use them as primitive man did: welcoming the visions they provided not as fantasies, but as intimations of a different, and important, level of reality."

—BRIAN INGLIS, JOURNALIST, HISTORIAN, AND TV PRESENTER

"People are unwinding, and they're relaxing. But they're also able to think and maybe analyze, or think clearly, pull back and see the macro, maybe make some changes in their lives. I think that cannabis really is more of a psychotherapeutic drug."

—JULIE HOLLAND, MD

"I've had some people offer up their couch for the night, or a place to wash some clothes. I think that's just an incredible thing to do for someone you don't know. Stoners are so generous."

—DAN GERVAIS, ACTIVIST
(PLANNING A CROSS-COUNTRY
AWARENESS WALK)

"Herb is a thing that will give you a little time to yourself so you can live if you use it."

—BOB MARLEY

"You would not wonder if you used this herb yourself. You might find that smoke blown out cleared your mind of shadows within. Anyway, it gives patience, to listen to error without anger."

—GANDALF IN J. R. R. TOLKIEN,
UNFINISHED TALES

"For the realized consciousness this world is no other than paradise, and its bliss and pleasures are all permitted."

—PETER LAMBORN WILSON

"There will come a time when people will recognize that this is a wonder drug of our times."

—LESTER GRINSPOON, MD

"I think the ratio, R, of the time to sense the dose taken to the time required to take an excessive dose is an important quantity. R is very large for LSD (which I've never taken) and reasonably short for cannabis. Small values of R should be one measure of the safety of psychedelic drugs. When cannabis is legalized, I hope to see this ratio as one of the parameters printed on the pack."

—CARL SAGAN

HIGH CREDENTIALS: CARL SAGAN

If we were all stoned, Sagan's R variable would make sense. Whenever someone makes a claim that stoners aren't productive members of society, respond with three simple words: Carl Fucking Sagan. A renowned and brilliant astronomer and astrophysicist (and stoner), Sagan cowrote and narrated *Cosmos,* one of the best documentary series to watch while stoned. Let Sagan's mellow, Kermit-the-Frog voice help you wind down from your day, pass out, and absorb slightly dated facts about the universe while you sleep.

"It's time to close the clinic in the shoebox under my bed."

—JON STEWART, *THE DAILY SHOW*

"The Greeks, who were much better at holding contradictory ideas in their minds than we are, understood that intoxication could be divine or wretched, a ceremony of human communion or madness, depending on the care taken in handling its magic."

—MICHAEL POLLAN, *THE BOTANY OF DESIRE*

"Soon I will control the world, a great big beautiful stoned world, with pot smoke clouds and oceans of bong water. And is there really anything so wrong with that?"

—MICHELLE MAIS AS EVIL BONG
IN *EVIL BONG*

"I could smoke weed every second of every day."

—JONAH HILL AS JONAH,
KNOCKED UP

"At the United Nations today, every nation has agreed on every proposal for the first time in history . . . and they're still trying to find out who put the grass in the air conditioner."

—DICK MARTIN REMEMBERING A
LAUGH-IN JOKE, *THEY'LL NEVER
PUT THAT ON THE AIR: AN ORAL
HISTORY OF TABOO-BREAKING
TV COMEDY*

"Could you imagine anything more dada than me as president? O but what to do about foreign affairs, how would Russia take to me? Actually, I'd go to Khrushchev with a stick of marijuana and together lie down listen to Bach as though we were dead to the world."

—GREGORY CORSO, *AN ACCIDEN-
TAL AUTOBIOGRAPHY*

"When you smoke the herb, it reveals you to yourself."

—BOB MARLEY

"Do you have any weed? . . . Just enough to get me baked for, like, a week. . . . I'm taking a vacation next week. . . . I'm not going anywhere, I'm going to stay in my apartment. I want to be baked the whole time."

—JANE LYNCH AS PAULA IN *THE
40 YEAR OLD VIRGIN* (EXTENDED
DVD VERSION)

"All I want, Santa Claus, is two fat bitches and a bag of weed and two bags of chips to give to the fat bitches."

—MIKE EPPS AS DAY-DAY, *FRI-
DAY AFTER NEXT*

FINE FUMES: CHRISTMAS KUSH

If you're the type to get excited when Starbucks rolls out the gingerbread lattes, then you should check out this holi-*dank*. This indica is said to hit you like a fat man falling down a chimney: *Wham!* And then you get presents!

"If you were to have marijuana free to be sold, a whole lot of pharmaceutical drugs would not be sold anymore."

—GARRETT MORRIS

"I've planted marijuana in community gardens all over the city, and it hasn't hurt anyone."

—MICHAEL GROSS AS A FORMER PARKS AND RECREATION DIRECTOR ON *PARKS AND RECREATION*

"My doctor prescribes it now. Heard you were sick too."

—MICHAEL ANGARANO AS SID, *LORDS OF DOGTOWN*

A place of fellowship, a place where people can get their medicine, relax, enjoy music. You have to have good music."

—JOHN SINCLAIR, POET AND ACTIVIST (PITCHING A MICHIGAN COMPASSION CENTER)

"You've been seeing a psychiatrist for fifteen years. You should smoke some o' this. You'd be off the couch in no time."

—DIANE KEATON AS ANNIE IN *ANNIE HALL*

"The idea that it can alleviate suffering and cancer in children alone should be a call to arms."

—RICHARD BELZER

"Cannabis is the only drug that decreases nausea and vomiting and also increases appetite. Also, I think, people sleep better, and a little bit of euphoria, I don't find, is a negative thing in people that are facing malignant diagnoses."

—DONALD ABRAMS, MD

"Because of the marijuana, my last two courses of chemotherapy were almost nausea-free. There was only one problem; I had to become a criminal to do this."

—RICHARD BROOKHISER, JOURNALIST

Jackie Treehorn (Ben Gazzara): New technology permits us to do very exciting things in interactive erotic software. Wave of the future, Dude. One hundred percent electronic!

The Dude (Jeff Bridges): Yeah well, I still jerk off manually.

—*THE BIG LEBOWSKI*

"Hi, come on in! Drugs to the right, hookers to the left."

—MICHAEL DUDIKOFF AS RYKO IN BACHELOR PARTY

"No one cares if you smoke a joint or not."

—ARNOLD SCHWARZENEGGER

"Every time you buy pot from Mexico or Colombia, you're putting an American out of work. We of the American Dope Growers Union support ourselves by growing marijuana in American soil."

—LARAINE NEWMAN AS A UNION MEMBER ON SATURDAY NIGHT LIVE

"I still believe some people should try drugs. In fact, some people should stay stoned all the time."

—DAVID CARRADINE

"Bring the brothers home and sisters home now. Legalize marijuana, and take all that money and invest it in teachers and education, and you will see a transformation in America. It is what is gonna like reunite us into people saying, 'Oh my God, now we can afford not to be paranoid.'"

—CARLOS SANTANA

George Lopez: Has my party bus become the Canna-bus?

Snoop Dogg: In so many words, we will be liftin', spliftin', and I'll be shiftin'.

—LOPEZ TONIGHT

"Herb is the healing of the nation."

—BOB MARLEY

"Everybody must get stoned."

—SHIA LABEOUF, VIA T-SHIRT

CHAPTER 14

MIXED WEEDIA

"The cannabis experience has greatly improved my appreciation for art, a subject which I had never much appreciated before."

—Carl Sagan

The average stoner has so many more options for entertainment than the average bro: Bob Ross marathons, Wagnerian opera, *Frasier* reruns, Jackson Pollack exhibits, Phish concerts, any Tim Burton film. For stoners the medium is the message—up in smoke!

Unfortunately, our memories of these transcendent experiences may be foggy. Maybe it was the pot-buttered popcorn on top of the fatties. Good times.

Here are some mellow ruminations on the nature of high art to jog your memory.

"Words must surely be counted among the most powerful drugs man ever invented."

—LEO ROSTEN,
WRITER AND HUMORIST

"Why write I still all one, ever the same,
    And keep invention in a noted weed. . . ."

—WILLIAM SHAKESPEARE,
"SONNET 76"

"Sanity and happiness are an impossible combination."

—MARK TWAIN

"Heaven bless hashish, if its dreams end like this!"

—LOUISA MAY ALCOTT,
PERILOUS PLAY

"It's about time that a movie where a man urinates in his own face is on the same top-ten list as *Munich* and *Syriana*. It's nice to know that some of the people who vote for these things smoke marijuana."

—JUDD APATOW

"*High Times* magazine . . . is like a notch intellectually below *Highlights* for children. I mean, they're both great to read when you're baked, but come on. You know?"

—DAVID CROSS

"Brad doesn't smoke while he's acting. And I don't smoke while I'm directing."

—QUENTIN TARANTINO

"It's about time that we got animated because we've been doing animation without the animation for years."

—CHEECH MARIN

"The way we handle dope is on an innocuous cartoon level."

—TOMMY CHONG

"I would define *Pineapple Express* as a love story between a dealer and his client."

—JAMES FRANCO

"It's great to be doing a movie where Cheech and I never have to get out of bed or be on camera."

—TOMMY CHONG

"I didn't realize this, but weed is considered a genre. A weed movie's like a horror movie or a sci-fi movie. To [studios] it's a genre that only some people like. Which we just never thought of."

—SETH ROGEN

POT SPOTS: IBIZA

Ibiza has some history with stoner cinema: It was the host of the first ever World Marijuana Film Festival. This island is like the Miami Beach of Spain, so expect parties, expect weed, and expect people in better shape than you. Even though there are efforts to make the island more "family friendly," it still maintains a relaxed atmosphere for toking.

"I was watching *True Romance* back in the late '90s on laserdisc, and I thought, 'Brad Pitt is so funny as this pothead character but there's only one scene. I kind of wish there was a whole movie about that guy.'"

—JUDD APATOW

HIGH CREDENTIALS: BRAD PITT

Pitt is the most revered stoner (possibly former stoner) in Hollywood, winning the respect and admiration of Bill Maher and Quentin Tarantino, and having surely smoked with Juliette Lewis, Jennifer Aniston, and Angelina Jolie. The dude has kids, fame, and money, and we can only assume it's thanks to the bud. If he had passed on a pass back in his formative years, we might be stuck with William B. Pitt, Oklahoma City's most mediocre financial analyst, instead of our stoner star.

"The truth would have been pot smoking, a lot of drinking, and more sex."

—JUDD APATOW (ABOUT *FREAKS AND GEEKS* AND NETWORK TELEVISION)

"I think Seth [Rogen] drunkenly sold the idea for part two to the executives at the wrap party."

—JAMES FRANCO (ON A POTENTIAL *PINEAPPLE EXPRESS* SEQUEL)

"Does it matter if that was vodka or water in the glass? I'd get angry!"

—PETER FONDA (REACTING TO BEING ASKED IF THE WEED SMOKED IN *EASY RIDER* WAS REAL)

"Marijuana serves the same purpose in *Nine to Five* as it does in *The Breakfast Club*. Acquaintances find themselves in an unpleasant situation . . . smoke marijuana together, and become friends as a result."

—DENNIS P. GRADY, *BEYOND THE STARS*, VOL. 3

"I would have to have a puff off a joint before every take. I'd run out to the bathroom and come back."

—DYAN CANNON

"Other people have speculated that I write on drugs, but the truth is I have never written anything not completely sober because it would be impossible for me not to write that way."

—CHARLIE KAUFMAN

"To put us in the same category as a *Saw IV* is just not accurate. These people smoke pot and what do they do? They giggle a little bit and then they bake."

—NANCY MEYERS (ON *IT'S COMPLICATED*'S R RATING)

Iris (Jodie Foster): Are you a narc?
Travis Bickle (Robert De Niro): Do I look like a narc?
Iris: Yeah.
Travis: I am a narc.

—*TAXI DRIVER*

HIGH CREDENTIALS: NANCY MEYERS

Though not an admitted stoner, Meyers did pot smokers a serious solid when she showed the ever-classy Meryl Streep getting high on screen in *It's Complicated*. Myers wrote, directed, and produced the romantic comedy, which showed the world not all pot smokers are unemployed, munchie-crazed slackers. Sometimes, they're Meryl Streep! And Alec Baldwin! And John Krasinski!

"It's a device used to show recklessness."

—JANEANE GAROFALO
(ON SMOKING WEED IN
VARIOUS MEDIA)

Alison (Katherine Heigl): I'm sorry I told you to fuck your bong.
Ben (Seth Rogen): It's okay. I didn't.

—*KNOCKED UP*

Tom (Jason Flemyng): No can do.
Nick the Greek (Stephen Marcus): What's that? A place near Kathmandu? Meet me half way, mate.

—*LOCK, STOCK AND TWO SMOKING BARRELS*

"He's wound up like an eight-day clock! One too many giggle sticks."

—ANA GASTEYER AS MAE COLEMAN IN *REEFER MADNESS: THE MOVIE MUSICAL*

Harold (John Cho): I'm not joining the Mile High Club with you.
Kumar (Kal Penn): What about the Really High Club?

—*HAROLD AND KUMAR ESCAPE FROM GUANTANAMO BAY*

"Marijuana is not a drug. I used to suck dick for coke. That's an addiction man. You ever suck some dick for marijuana? . . . I didn't think so."

—BOB SAGET AS A COCAINE
ADDICT IN *HALF BAKED*

"If Margaret Mead at her age smoked grass, she'd have one hell of a trip."

—MICHAEL JETER AS L. RON
BUMQUIST IN *FEAR AND LOATH-
ING IN LAS VEGAS*

"I'm fat, black, can't dance, and I have two gay fathers. People have been messing with me my whole life. I learned a long time ago that there's no sense getting all riled up every time a bunch of idiots give you a hard time. In the end, the universe tends to unfold as it should. Plus I have a really large penis. That keeps me happy."

—GARY ANTHONY WILLIAMS AS
TARIK, *HAROLD AND KUMAR GO
TO WHITE CASTLE*

"Don't 'ugh' me, Greek boy! How is it your fucking stupid, soon-to-be dead friends thought they might be able to steal my cannabis, and then sell it back to me?"

—VAS BLACKWOOD AS RORY
BREAKER IN *LOCK, STOCK AND
TWO SMOKING BARRELS*

Kumar (Kal Penn): Hang on a second, nurse. What we should probably use is marijuana. That'll sufficiently sedate the patient for surgery.
Nurse (Ryan Reynolds): Marijuana? But Why?
Kumar: We don't have time for questions. We need marijuana now, as much of it as possible! Like a big bag of it.

—*HAROLD AND KUMAR GO TO
WHITE CASTLE*

"The Dude abides."

—JEFF BRIDGES AS THE DUDE
IN *THE BIG LEBOWSKI*

"It was absolutely about pot."

—BILLIE JOE ARMSTRONG OF
GREEN DAY (WHEN BILL MAHER
ASKED WHAT THEIR BAND NAME
REFERENCED)

"What did you expect? 'Welcome, Sonny'? 'Make yourself at home'? 'Marry my daughter'? You've got to remember that these are just simple farmers. These are people of the land. The common clay of the new West. You know . . . morons."

—GENE WILDER AS JIM,
AFTER BLAZING UP IN *BLAZING
SADDLES*

"If John Lennon is deported, I'm leaving too . . . with my musicians . . . and my marijuana."

—ART GARFUNKEL

"Grass was really influential in a lot of our changes, especially with the writers. And because they were writing different material, we were playing differently. We were expanding in all areas of our lives, opening up to a lot of different attitudes."

—RINGO STARR, *THE BEATLES
ANTHOLOGY*

"This country was founded by free-thinking great minds, but the breed is a diminishing one. We should be thankful that Lennon wants to make these shores his home. Since his spirit will always live with us, it's really pointless to banish its physical manifestation."

—CLIVE DAVIS

HIGH CREDENTIALS: JOHN LENNON

All four Beatles were blazed, but Lennon, prone to activism, was perhaps the most passionate about marijuana and its legalization. Some people even believe he was assassinated because of it. While that can't be proven, what is certain is that pot nearly got him deported, a move pushed by Nixon, who, had he not found himself resigning from his own scandal, might have succeeded. Luckily Gerald Ford was a little chiller.

"The Beatles didn't write great songs because they smoked pot. The Beatles were geniuses who happened to get high. It's not like monkeys and typewriters. It's not like you get high enough and then *Sgt. Pepper* will just come out of you."

—PAUL F. TOMPKINS ON *LEWIS BLACK'S ROOT OF ALL EVIL*

"I started smoking grass because it was either that or some kind of medication which I didn't want to take. This time last year I was a complete and utter pot-head. I know it's lunacy but the grass really helped me with the lyrics.

I'd know there was something I really wanted to say but I wouldn't know how to say it. So I'd have a few drags and stand behind the mike and in a few minutes I'd be there. It's bad because I don't want to smoke but I can't see myself giving up grass as a writer."

—GEORGE MICHAEL, *GEORGE MICHAEL: IN HIS OWN WORDS*

"In every band, at least half of the musicians smoked reefers. I'm not going to list names; I'd have to include some of those most prominent then in popular music."

—MALCOLM X, *THE AUTOBIOGRAPHY OF MALCOLM X*

"Sorry if I'm a singer, not a saint."

—WAGNER CARRILHO, U.K. TV PERSONALITY

"We have a lot of stoners in our band, so to have marijuana still be illegal is ridiculous."

—COURTNEY TAYLOR-TAYLOR OF THE DANDY WARHOLS

"I'm Peggy Olson, and I want to smoke some marijuana."

—ELISABETH MOSS ON *MAD MEN*

"We fucked up all the big ones—Monterey Pop, Woodstock, Egypt. At Monterey we came on between The Who and Hendrix. The Who blew everyone away, broke their instruments, and then we came out and went, 'Plink, plink, plink,' and then Hendrix came out and ended up lighting his guitar on fire—we were pathetic."

—JERRY GARCIA, *THIRTY-NINE YEARS OF SHORT-TERM MEMORY LOSS*

"If you stay with the song long enough, then you start to realize it's not about marijuana. It's actually about freedom and living your life."

—JOHN MAYER (ON HIS SONG "WHO SAYS")

Anita Miller (Zooey Deschanel): Simon and Garfunkel is poetry!

Elaine Miller (Frances McDormand): Yes it's poetry. It's the poetry of drugs and promiscuous sex. Look at the picture on the cover, they're on pot.

—*ALMOST FAMOUS*

"I'm seldom in Muskogee."

—MERLE HAGGARD

Michael (Jason Bateman): My mom is very stressed out, and she needs something I can't give her. Maybe a little afternoon delight.

Narrator (Ron Howard): Oscar thought that Michael was referring to a particular brand of cannabis named "Afternoon Delight," a strain famous for slowing behavior.

Oscar (Jeffrey Tambor): Well, sure. The question is, which way do I try to get it in her?

Michael: I don't need any details.

Oscar: Maybe I'll put it in her brownie.

Michael: Hey!

—*ARRESTED DEVELOPMENT*

"We can't do this in here. Ritchie breathes this air. Let's go out to the garage. Okay? He never goes in there. He saw a rake in there once. He thought it was a mummy with a machine gun."

—JULIA LOUIS-DREYFUS AS CHRISTINE ON *THE NEW ADVENTURES OF OLD CHRISTINE*

"That ain't red gravy. That's what you call 'marijuana sauce.'"

—MAX BAER JR. AS JETHRO ON *THE BEVERLY HILLBILLIES* (ALMOST IDENTIFYING MARINARA SAUCE CORRECTLY)

"Boris is so dumb, he thinks a little pot is Tupperware for midgets."

—JO ANNE WORLEY ON *LAUGH-IN*

"Mr. White? Are you smoking weed? Oh my God! Wait a minute, is that my weed? What the hell, man? Make yourself at home, why don't you?"

—AARON PAUL AS JESSE PINK-MAN ON *BREAKING BAD*

"I don't know where the John Davidson staff and the great middle-American viewing audience thought Al's [the Hippy-Dippy Weatherman] weirdness came from, whether he sipped a little wine or whether they just thought Al was dumb as a brick, an early version of Forrest Gump. But I knew Al's jokes were written from a pot mentality."

—GEORGE CARLIN (ON HIS CHARACTER), *LAST WORDS*

"What is the different types of hash out there? We all know that it's called the bionic, the bomb, the puff, the blow, the black, the herb, the sensi, the chronic, the sweet Mary Jane, the shit, ganja, split, reefer, the bad, the Buddha, the homegrown, the ill, the Maui-Maui, the method, pot, lethal, turbo, tie, shake, skunk, stress, whacky, weed, glaze, the boot, dime bag, Scooby Doo, bob, bogey, backyard boogie. But what is the other terms for it?"

—SASHA BARON COHEN AS ALI G ON *DA ALI G SHOW*

POT SPOTS: IOWA

Iowa doesn't get enough credit, sitting there in Mid-America. They got gay marriage, and now they're going for pot. It's a cool place, but you don't even have to be in Iowa to experience it. The fine folks at the newspaper *Iowa Farmer Today* have put a corn cam up on their website. They describe it better than I ever could: "An image of a corn field that is updated every 15 minutes." If that wasn't made for stoners . . . then, I'm afraid of Iowa.

"I'm not a dealer, I'm a mother who happens to distribute illegal products through a sham bakery set up by my ethically questionable CPA and his crooked lawyer friend."

—MARY-LOUISE PARKER AS
NANCY BOTWIN ON *WEEDS*

"Reverend" Jim (Christopher Lloyd): Yeah, I did some drugs, though probably not as many as you think. How many drugs do you think I did?

Elaine Nardo (Marilu Henner): A lot.

"Reverend" Jim: Wow! Right on the nose!

—*TAXI*

Nancy Botwin (Mary-Louise Parker): People got stoned for *The Passion of the Christ*? That's disturbing.

Josh Wilson (Justin Chatwin): It's not as disturbing as seeing it not stoned. Religion my ass. It's a straight up snuff film.

—*WEEDS*

Tim (Simon Pegg): Daisy . . . it's gonna be okay. Now have a big toke of this South African drug's reefer-style spliff doobie.

Daisy (Jessica Hynes): I don't know. It might make me paranoid.

—*SPACED*

"Homer, for your eyes, the best tonic is chronic. You're not afraid, are you?"

—HARRY SHEARER AS DR. HIB-
BERT ON *THE SIMPSONS*

FINE FUMES: DURBAN POISON
This extreme sativa put South Africa on the map for stoners. Residents are quick to boast about how inexpensive and copious their famed headies are. It's suckworthy for foreigners, though, since the Poison is a lot less common outside South Africa. We're all hoping the recent World Cup provided opportunities for some covert exports and that soon, we can all score.

Logan Echolls (Jason Dohring): Didn't your dad say that the cigar store's a front for drug dealers? I mean, that's gotta be something.

Veronica Mars (Kristen Bell): Or not. Sometimes a cigar store is just a cigar store.

—VERONICA MARS

Cleveland (Mike Henry): Did you eat the brownies in the back of the freezer?

Cleveland Jr. (Kevin Michael Richardson): No.

Cleveland (Mike Henry): Good, don't 'cause they're your dad's for when he goes to concerts.

—THE CLEVELAND SHOW

"If you're sitting here tonight thinking, I want to get high with a dude who's been on TV a bunch in a parking lot next to a Del Taco, that is an achievable goal."

—BRIAN POSEHN

"If you don't grow it, I'm going to tell on you."

—DANA SNYDER AS MASTER SHAKE ON *AQUA TEEN HUNGER FORCE*

"Towelie, over the past few months I have watched you go from an ancillary character with a few amusing catch phrases to a dried-out spooge rag, covered in the jizz of a thousand older men."

—MATT STONE AS KYLE ON *SOUTH PARK*

"Let me get high. I know I can remember if I get high."

—VERNON CHATMAN AS TOWELIE ON *SOUTH PARK*

"It's a little ironic . . . here you're looking at an actor who's starred in two very popular marijuana films: *Half Baked* and *Bio-Dome*, and here I am bringing a faith-based conservative perspective to this issue. . . . It's a very simple reality. Marijuana leads to doing worse things."

—STEPHEN BALDWIN

CHAPTER 15

REEFER MADNESS

"Here we have a drug that is not like opium. Opium has all of the good of Dr. Jekyll and all the evil of Mr. Hyde. This drug is entirely the monster Hyde, the harmful effect of which cannot be measured."

—Harry J. Anslinger

The only thing we have to fear is fear itself . . . and marijuana, sex before marriage, Ouija boards, terrorists, and older men who walk near playgrounds. Creating fear is a wonderful way to control people, like when you tell your roommate you won't call your dealer if he doesn't do the dishes. So yeah, imagine you're a pharmaceutical giant or someone in the forestry industry and this cute, fun little plant comes along and gets all your customers hot and heavy. . . . You're going to freak the flip out!

Solution? Make that cute, little plant seem like the *Cloverfield* monster. (I still haven't seen that movie.)

Let's take a look at how some of the more passionate anti-marijuana messaging has (hopefully) become a little less scary and way more entertaining.

"It creates delusions of grandeur and breaks down the will power and makes the addict ready for any crime, even murder. The last stage is a depression during which suicide is often contemplated or even accomplished."

—IDA B. WISE SMITH, PRESIDENT OF THE WOMAN'S CHRISTIAN TEMPERANCE UNION, 1935

"Now marijuana is found to be the introductory drug to much of the heroinism in young people in the United States."

—HARRY J. ANSLINGER AND WILLIAM F. TOMPKINS, *THE TRAFFIC IN NARCOTICS*

"If the hideous monster Frankenstein came face to face with the monster marijuana he would drop dead of fright."

—HARRY J. ANSLINGER

"It's a fact. No one ever got cancer from pot. But it's also a fact that no one ever dropped out of school because they were hung up on tobacco. And no one who just finished smoking a cigarette ever forgot she was driving a car as she tripped out on the beauty of a back-road nature trip."

—SONNY BONO, *MARIJUANA* (1968)

"'Bad news' isn't the half of it. Here are the facts; when the smoke hits the brain, the cells start dying. This process causes impaired judgment and hallucinations and a lot of other wonderful things."

—DANNY MASTERSON AS HYDE, *THAT '70S SHOW*

"Now, what I am about to show you next may shock and educate you. Hold onto your values as we step through the looking glass into a hippie pot party."

—HANK AZARIA AS CHIEF WIGGUM ON *THE SIMPSONS*

172   THE QUOTABLE STONER

"I say I was half addicted . . . because two of me believe, as a loyal government employee, that the old government publications claiming marijuana is addicting must be true or the government wouldn't have printed them. Fortunately, the other two of me know that it isn't addicting, so I don't go through very bad withdrawal when it's scarce."

—ROBERT SHEA AND ROBERT ANTON WILSON, *THE ILLUMINATUS! TRILOGY*

"I am extremely troubled that at a time when teenage drug abuse is doubling . . . a television show of the caliber of *Murphy Brown* would portray marijuana as medicine. It is not medicine. . . . More dangerously, the show sends the message to our children that marijuana must be OK because it's medicine."

—THOMAS CONSTANTINE, FORMER DEA ADMINISTRATOR

"I am unto myself a statistic—the only statistic I need . . . twenty-three years of living with gutter hypes and junkies. I have thousands of friends—if you will. They're all junkies, and there isn't one—not one—who didn't start, smoking marijuana."

—FLORRIE FISHER

"Addicts may often develop a delirious rage during which they are temporarily and violently insane; this insanity may take the form of a desire for self-destruction or a persecution complex to be satisfied only by the commission of some heinous crime."

—HARRY J. ANSLINGER

HIGH CREDENTIALS: FLORENCE "FLORRIE" FISHER

Fisher is a major inspiration for *Strangers with Candy*'s principal protagonist, and often antagonist, Jerri Blank. Florrie, like Jerri, has seen it all, and tried it all. Some of Jerri's best lines come right from Fisher's speeches to high school students about the perils of drugs ("I was thrown from a horse and I had a laminectomy"). Videos of Florrie's speeches surfaced in recent years on the Internet. Major props to Stephen Colbert, Paul Dinello, and Amy Sedaris, who got their hands on them in the pre-YouTube days.

"Once a newspaper touches a story, the facts are lost forever, even to the protagonists."

—NORMAN MAILER

"Marijuana is the flame. Heroin is the fuse. LSD is the bomb."

—JACK WEBB AS JOE FRIDAY ON *DRAGNET*

"Marijuana is a narcotic, medically and legally. It never did anyone any good, and does everyone a lot of harm."

—JACK WEBB AS JOE FRIDAY ON *DRAGNET*

"Scientists don't smoke pot. We do, and that's the difference. All I'm saying is that if you still want to smoke pot, be prepared to spend a lot of time laughing with your friends."

—PAUL DINELLO AS MR. JELLI-NECK ON *STRANGERS WITH CANDY*

"I married a man. This boy—he smoked marijuana. This was his only crime. He was a young kid. He had two years of college. And you know what I did? I made a pimp out of him. An 18-karat pimp. I was a call girl. I was young, I was fly, I was pretty. And I was out selling my body, kept going to jail. And you know ten years later I had to be ten dollars cheaper, and I wasn't a call girl. I became a madam. Then I became a street whore. Then I've been in every department store. My mug was in every post office. It isn't now, thank God, but it was."

—FLORRIE FISHER

"Do your children enjoy jazz music? For I am here to tell you that Cab Calloway, Dizzy Gillespie, Duke Ellington, and the whole weed-blowing ginger-colored lot are merely masquerading as musicians and are, in fact, agents of evil. Reefer slows down the smoker's sense of time, allowing him to squeeze in unnecessary grace notes, giving this voodoo music the power to hypnotize white women into indulging in acts of unspeakable degradation."

—ALAN CUMMING AS THE LEC-TURER IN *REEFER MADNESS: THE MOVIE MUSICAL*

"Jazz grew up next door to crime, so to speak. Clubs of dubious reputation were, for a long time, the only places where it could be heard."

—Harry Anslinger,
The Protectors

"I have six people that I count as friends who use marijuana, and true, they never did graduate to heroin. You know why? Because on marijuana, they committed crimes of passion and were electrocuted before they got a chance to get hooked on horse."

—Florrie Fisher

"*Know your dope fiend! Your life may depend on it!* You will not be able to see his eyes because of Tea-Shades, but his knuckles will be white from inner tension, and his pants will be crusted with semen from constantly jacking off when he can't find a rape victim."

—Donald Morrow as the
Drug Film Narrator in *Fear
and Loathing in Las Vegas*

"I have this one last hit of doobie reefer, and then I'm done for. I never wanted it to end this way: a pot-addicted prostitute, missing a lung, and fueling terrorism."

—Kristen Schaal (stand-up
monologue)

"The motion picture you are about to witness may startle you. It would not have been possible, otherwise, to sufficiently emphasize the frightful toll of the new drug menace, which is destroying the youth of America in alarmingly increasing numbers. Marihuana is that drug—a violent narcotic—an unspeakable scourge—The Real Public Enemy Number One!"

—*Tell Your Children
(Reefer Madness)* (opening
crawl)

"I really remember . . . that people camped out everywhere, and the fact everybody expected it might turn into a big nightmare with all sorts of hassles because back in those days everybody was smoking pot and taking acid. Actually, there was not one incident."

—JOHNNY RIVERS (ON THE MON-
TEREY POP FESTIVAL)

POT SPOTS: BURNING MAN
Festivals make the rest of the year worth bearing. Burning Man dominates because if you're a stoner, you like to burn things, from the tiniest of roaches, to the largest wooden man. Though there are increasing restrictions and regulations each year as the festival grows in popularity, it's still a chance to exercise artistic freedom in a huge open space . . . and weed abounds.

"Bill, I'm going to ask you a straightforward question, and I'd like to have a straightforward answer. Isn't it true that you have—perhaps unwillingly—acquired a certain harmful habit, through association with certain undesirable people?"

—JOSEF FORTE AS DR. CAR-
ROLL IN *TELL YOUR CHILDREN*
(REEFER MADNESS)

"They're Marihuana weed, a devilish narcotic; and if you smoke them, you go bughouse, loco, and want to raise h— in general."

—A TITLE CARD IN *NOTCH NUM-
BER ONE* (1924)

"He is hopelessly and incurably insane, a condition caused by the drug marijuana to which he was addicted. It is recommended, your honor, that the defendant be placed in an institution for the criminally insane for the rest of his natural life."

—UNCREDITED ATTORNEY IN
TELL YOUR CHILDREN
(REEFER MADNESS)

"More vicious, more deadly even than these soul-destroying drugs, is the menace of marihuana!"

—JOSEF FORTE AS DR. CAR-
ROLL IN TELL YOUR CHILDREN
(REEFER MADNESS)

"That was marijuana you were smoking! It's worse than cocaine! . . . See those punks over there, Marge? They were high a few minutes ago—up in the clouds. Now they're getting low. Pretty soon they'll be mean, ready to commit murder. Marijuana's called 'the murder weed.'"

—BLANCHE MEHAFFEY AS
FLORENCE IN THE WAGES OF
SIN (1938)

"The actual marijuana smoke is four to six times more carcinogenic than your regular cigarettes."

—DR. HAROLD C. URSCHEL, III

"Marijuana: the excuse for anything."

—MARYJANE (1968) THEATRICAL
TRAILER

"There is not a shred of scientific evidence that smoked marijuana is useful or needed."

—U.S. DRUG CZAR, GEN. BARRY
MCCAFFREY

"In Scientology, we have the only successful drug rehabilitation program in the world. It's called Narconon."

—TOM CRUISE

"We've got to compete with China, and if everybody's stoned, how the hell are we going to make it?"

—JERRY BROWN,
CALIFORNIA GOVERNOR

"I've read the pamphlets; today it's marijuana, tomorrow I'm a crack whore."

—GINA GERSHON AS JACKI IN
PREY FOR ROCK & ROLL

"That was no insult, stupid. That was a proposition."

—CARLETON YOUNG AS BRUCE
IN THE WAGES OF SIN

"If the founding fathers had been on marijuana, they never would have written the Constitution."

—NELSON ROCKEFELLER

Sam (Tim Meadows): No Dewey, you don't want this. Get out of here.

Dewey Cox (John C. Reilly): You know what, I don't want no hangover. I can't get no hangover.

Sam: It doesn't give you a hangover.

Dewey: Wha—I get addicted to it or something?

Sam: It's not habit forming.

Dewey: Oh, well, I don't know. I don't want to overdose on it.

Sam: You can't O.D. on it.

Dewey: It's not gonna make me want to have sex, is it?

Sam: It makes sex even better.

Dewey: Sounds kind of expensive.

Sam: It's the cheapest drug there is. . . . You don't want it.

—WALK HARD

FINE FUMES: TOM CRUISE PURPLE

If you ever want to jump up and down on Oprah's couch and need something to blame, this could be the strain for you. It's said to cause intense and powerful hallucinations. Tom Cruise wasn't too pleased to hear that his maniacally laughing face served as the product's label. Know who was? Everyone else ever.

"You want to have two guys making out in front of your four-year-old? It's okay with them. A guy smoking a joint, blowing the smoke into your little kid's face? Okay with them. And I'm not exaggerating here. This is exactly what the secular movement stands for."

—BILL O'REILLY

Sid Hudgens (Danny DeVito): "It's Christmas Eve in the City of Angels and while decent citizens sleep the sleep of the righteous, hopheads prowl for marijuana, not knowing that a man is coming to stop them! Celebrity crimestopper Jack Vincennes, scourge of grass-hoppers and dope fiends everywhere!" Ya like it, Jackie boy?
Jack Vincennes (Kevin Spacey): Yeah, subtle.

—*L.A. CONFIDENTIAL*

"The more you can increase fear of drugs and crime, welfare mothers, immigrants and aliens, the more you control all the people."

—NOAM CHOMSKY

"What's up, Doc, is your life, if you don't get off those drugs."

—JEFF BERGMAN AS BUGS BUNNY IN *CARTOON ALL-STARS TO THE RESCUE*

"We first fought the heathens in the name of religion, then Communism, and now in the name of drugs and terrorism. . . . Our excuses for world domination always change."

—SYSTEM OF A DOWN

"They've been teaching the children and giving the children a bunch of lies and Mother Goose rhymes. . . . You tell them Jack and Jill went up the hill after some water. I tell them the water don't run up hill. You tell them that Mary had a little lamb. I tell them, 'Wasn't the doctor surprised!'"

—MOMS MABLEY

"'Rock Against Drugs,' what a name. Somebody was high when they came up with that title. It's like 'Christians Against Christ.' Rock created drugs."

—SAM KINISON

"Even if one takes every reefer madness allegation of the prohibitionists at face value, marijuana prohibition has done far more harm to far more people than marijuana ever could."

—WILLIAM F. BUCKLEY, JR.

"The musician who uses 'reefers' finds that the musical beat seemingly comes to him quite slowly, thus allowing him to interpolate any number of improvised notes with comparative ease. While under the influence of marijuana, he does not realize that he is tapping the keys, with a furious speed impossible for one in a normal state of mind."

—HARRY J. ANSLINGER

"The more he needs the escape from reality or the pleasure of marijuana, the more he is becoming emotionally dependent, exactly as the square and unhip alcoholic adult does."

—SONNY BONO,
MARIJUANA (1968)

CHAPTER 16

WHO'S HIGHER?

"Right now I think it's in my interest, and ours perhaps and maybe in the interest of the greater good, for me to smoke a joint and calm down."

—Hunter S. Thompson interviewed on *Omnibus*

Who's higher? In an age where many celebrity stoners barely admit to using weed, and where some go so far as to publicly call it a "mistake"—hold me back!—it's a comfort to know some blazing stars are smoking up often and unapologetically. It's good to have role models—and *roll* models. Even though we haven't reached a day where all stoners can march proudly out of their hotbox closets, we've got a pretty impressive roster growing in that black light of fame.

It would be inaccurate—but still so fun—to say there's a competition for greatest cultural "highcon," so check out these claims to fame, and judge for yourself. Who's higher? And who's higher than you?

"I stayed up all night watching Cheech and Chong, getting my mind together."

—SNOOP DOGG (ON PREPARING FOR HIS ROLE ON *WEEDS*)

"I was doing *Fear Factor* and *The Man Show* and Jujutsu, smoking weed every fuckin' day!"

—JOE ROGAN

"My best friend Sasha's dad was Carl Sagan, the astronomer. He was the biggest pot smoker in the world and he was a genius."

—KIRSTEN DUNST

"When high on cannabis I discovered that there's somebody inside in those people we call mad."

—CARL SAGAN

"If somebody gives me a joint, I might smoke it, but I don't go after it."

—JOHN LENNON

"I totally smoked for a while and then I totally stopped. . . . Yeah, it really sucks remembering where I put stuff now. The whole first week I thought I was psychic."

—NICK SWARDSON

"There is an occasional celebratory jay, but it's not like a wake and bake scenario anymore at all."

—JACK BLACK

"Marijuana is like sex. If I don't do it every day, I get a headache."

—WILLIE NELSON

"If you got some chronic, now's the time to blaze that shit up. Obama smoked too. Make sure you're wakin' and bakin'. Stay smoking."

—SNOOP DOGG

HIGH CREDENTIALS: JIM BREUER

The man was born to play (and be) a stoner. Of course, *Half Baked* was his only real movie role, since we're still waiting for the Goat Boy feature to be greenlit. Apparently, Universal wanted the part of Brian in *Half Baked* to go Christian Slater, but Dave Chappelle fought for Breuer to get the role, saying that he wouldn't even need makeup to play the part!

"I used to smoke marijuana. But I'll tell you something. I would only smoke it in the late evening. Oh, occasionally the early evening, but usually the late evening. Or the mid-evening. Just the early evening, mid-evening and late evening. Occasionally, early afternoon, early mid-afternoon, or perhaps the late-mid-afternoon. Oh, sometimes the early-mid-late-early morning . . . but never at dusk! Never at dusk. I would never do that."

—STEVE MARTIN

"I use it to control the nausea which comes with the headaches."

—KAREEM ABDUL-JABBAR

"This is the way I look all the time. I'm not high."

—JIM BREUER

"I was introduced to pot by a Chinese jazz musician in Calgary, Canada, in 1957. He gave me a joint and a Lenny Bruce record and changed my life forever."

—TOMMY CHONG, *CHEECH & CHONG: THE UNAUTHORIZED AUTOBIOGRAPHY*

"We're not influenced by kids; they're not influenced by us. We're a minimal part of their lives compared to everything else. . . . Nowadays, no one really cares about marijuana as far as I can see."

—TOMMY CHONG

"I don't think of myself as a hip-hop artist. I think of myself as a rock star."

—SNOOP DOGG

"We were trying to be the Cheech and Chong of punk rock for a while. . . . Some of us still are the Cheech and Chong of punk rock in a lot of ways."

—BILLIE JOE ARMSTRONG OF GREEN DAY

"Purple Haze, Motherfuckers!"

—ADAM LAMBERT (TOKING ON STAGE IN AMSTERDAM)

FINE FUMES: PURPLE HAZE

Adam Lambert recently covered the Hendrix song, and forced us all to ask, "Do we like Adam Lambert now?" History leans to Hendrix inspiring the name of this deep purple sativa, not the other way around. While the original strain is probably long gone, its mutant descendants keep the really really uplifting legacy alive.

"I think it may have had something to do with the joint I smoked before I came on, but I didn't inhale. Doesn't count really."

—MADONNA (ON HER EARLIER *LATE SHOW* APPEARANCE)

"I go on little weedfests. I'm a pot-head. That's my drug of choice."

—Joseph Gordon-Levitt

"I only get ill when I give up drugs."

—Keith Richards

"Have you ever smoked endo? . . . You should."

—Madonna to David Letter-man on *The Late Show with David Letterman*

"So I come off the most produc-tive year of my professional career, yet it was the one through which I was blitzed. . . . I was joy-fully fucking stoned throughout."

—Kevin Smith, *SModcast*

HIGH CREDENTIALS: KEVIN SMITH
Dude hotboxes with his mom . . . and recorded it for us to enjoy. Enough said! But he's also pretty much the God of the View Askewniverse, the official reality where all the Jay and Silent Bob movies take place. And Smith is, of course, the expressive though silent Silent Bob.

"[Timothy] Leary can get a part of my mind that's kind of rusted shut grinding again, just by being around him and talking, 'cause that's where he works. He knows that area of the mind and the brain, and he knows the differ-ence between the two areas. He's a real master at getting your old wheel squeaking again."

—Ken Kesey

"I still smoke, but I've changed my habits a little bit. I smoke with a vaporizer; it's easier on my lungs. I have several of them."

—Willie Nelson

"I smoke marijuana sometimes a lot every day."

—Greer Barnes

"Effective today: NBC will stop paying for Andy Richter's medical marijuana and medical Jack Daniel's."

—CONAN O'BRIEN, *THE TONIGHT SHOW WITH CONAN O'BRIEN*

"It appears that a 'Hasheesh' mania has broken out among our Bohemians. Yesterday, Mark Twain and the 'Mouse-Trap' man [Tremenheere Lanyon Johns] were seen walking up Clay Street under the influence of the drug, followed by a 'star,' who was evidently laboring under a misapprehension as to what was the matter with them."

—*SAN FRANCISCO DRAMATIC CHRONICLE*

"So what if I'm smokin' weed onstage and doing what I gotta do? It's not me shooting nobody, stabbing nobody, killing nobody. It's a peaceful gesture and they have to respect that and appreciate that."

—SNOOP DOGG

"We all used to smoke weed all day instead of working, and we'd just play video games for months on end, but we all really wanted to work and make movies."

—SETH ROGEN

"The final grand transformation scene is a vision of magnificence such as no man could imagine unless he had eaten a barrel of hasheesh."

—MARK TWAIN

"Davis, I'm the Jerry Garcia of comedy."

—JOHN BELUSHI, *THIRTY-NINE YEARS OF SHORT-TERM MEMORY LOSS*

"Right now, I'm so high you're hallucinating."

—WILLIE NELSON, *A COLBERT CHRISTMAS*

"I think I'm high from pretending."

—STEPHEN COLBERT, *THE COLBERT REPORT*

"Once you've had Colombian, domestic just doesn't cut it anymore."

—WANDA SYKES, *YEAH, I SAID IT*

"I had experimented with other drugs, but marijuana was my drug of choice."

—BOBBY BROWN, *BOBBY BROWN: THE TRUTH, THE WHOLE TRUTH AND NOTHING BUT*

"On a day-to-day basis, I smoke at least ten blunts. . . . As soon as I wake up, before I even get dressed or do anything, I'm like . . . [inhales]."

—KRAYZIE BONE

"I'm sure Zach [Galifianakis] had his card with him. I know I'd like to have a card, Zach."

—WHOOPI GOLDBERG ON *THE JOY BEHAR SHOW*

"Medical marijuana makes me sick."

—P. J. O'ROURKE

Sarah Silverman: It's a little bit of pot. This isn't cigarettes.
Rod Steiger: I bought it . . . I had that when you were in diapers.
Sarah Silverman: That could have been any time in the past.

—*DINNER FOR FIVE* (DVD)

HIGH CREDENTIALS: SARAH SILVERMAN

Silverman is a pot-friendly comic and actress with a pot-friendly (and awesome) cable show. She said on *The View* that one of her favorite hobbies is pushing Barbara Walters's buttons—or trying to. At an awards show she passed Walters's table and declared rebelliously that she was going to smoke weed. Walters grabbed her arm, unfazed, and said, "Your mother and I are so proud."

"Prop. 19. You know how I stand on that. . . . Very high."

—Snoop Dogg

"I spend like . . . I maybe spend like $23,000 a week on weed."

—Krayzie Bone

"You smoke so much weed, though, you're like Willie Nelson Mandela."

—George Lopez to Snoop Dogg on *Lopez Tonight*

"When I was in England I experimented with marijuana a time or two, and I didn't like it and didn't inhale it, and never tried it again."

—President Bill Clinton

"I can't claim a Bill Clinton and say that I never inhaled."

—Sarah Palin

POT SPOTS: ALASKA
Possess and enjoy up to an ounce in private, and then jump on a helicopter and shoot some wolves. Maybe even fight a polar bear. Alaska offers stoner-tolerant adventures, though with only one person per square mile, finding a source for your sticky can be tricky.

"I'm on medical marijuana as we speak."

—Snoop Dogg

"[Bill Clinton] preferred, like many another marijuana enthusiast, to take his dope in the form of large handfuls of cookies and brownies."

—CHRISTOPHER HITCHENS, AUTHOR AND JOURNALIST

"Judge Thomas took several puffs on a marijuana cigarette in college and perhaps once in law school."

—WHITE HOUSE STATEMENT, 1991

"I have a reputation for giving unpopular answers at democratic debates. I never used marijuana. Sorry."

—JOE LIEBERMAN

"When I was a kid . . . I inhaled frequently. That was the point."

—BARACK OBAMA

"I've never taken any hard drugs. When I was a student, I took one or two puffs of marijuana but that was it."

—VERNON COAKER, U.K. MINISTER FOR DRUGS AND CRIME REDUCTION

HIGH CREDENTIALS: BARACK OBAMA

He inhaled. That was the point. Harry Anslinger, anti-marijuana propagandist extraordinaire is resting smugly in a grave, knowing that the first modern president to be unashamed of his reefer past is the black one. What has his country come to? Our answer: a much better place! Obama has said he won't devote resources to reversing marijuana laws, but also that he won't actively step up enforcement. For where we are in America right now, that's not so bad. Yes we cannabis!

"You bet I did. And I enjoyed it!"

—MICHAEL BLOOMBERG, NEW YORK CITY MAYOR

"Yes, grass and hash—no hard drugs. But the point is that I do what I feel like doing. I'm not on a health kick."

—ARNOLD SCHWARZENEGGER
(IN 1977)

"What was done with the Seed saved from the India Hemp last summer? It ought, all of it, to have been sown again; that not only a stock of seed sufficient for my own purposes might have been raised, but to have disseminated the seed to others; as it is more valuable than the common Hemp."

—GEORGE WASHINGTON

"That is not a drug. It's a leaf. My drug is pumping iron, trust me."

—ARNOLD SCHWARZENEGGER

"When [Dan Quayle] and Marilyn got married in 1972, I gave him a wedding present of some Afghanistan hashish and some Acapulco Gold."

—BRETT KIMBERLIN, CONVICTED DRUG AND EXPLOSIVES SMUGGLER

"[Smoking marijuana] was a sign that we were alive and in graduate school during that era."

—NEWT GINGRICH

"I wouldn't answer the marijuana question. You know why? 'Cause I don't want some little kid doing what I tried. You gotta understand, I want to be president, I want to lead. Do you want your little kid to say, 'Hey daddy, President Bush tried marijuana, I think I will'?"

—GEORGE W. BUSH

"It would be pretty hard for some drug guy to come into the White House and start offering it up, you know? . . . But I bet if they did, I hope I would say, 'Hey, get lost. We don't want any of that.'"

—GEORGE H. W. BUSH

"The whole point of 'just say no' is to try to reach out to people and say 'in the '60s, you may have experimented, in the '70s, you may have experimented.' It was a mistake. It wasn't an 'of course.'"

—NEWT GINGRICH

CHAPTER 17

WELCOME TO STONERVILLE

"Canada rocks. Primo weed, really good Chinese food."
—Allison Janney as Ms. Greenstein on *Weeds*

The world is totally awesome—wherever you go you find new people, new cultures, and most importantly, new places to smoke new weed. Sometimes life really is greener on the other side, so say goodbye to your couch and get out there, man! Vancouver, Amsterdam, the Emerald Triangle are all must-sees, and you never know just what you'll toke.

No need to bring along your stash when you visit these pot spots. After all, you have to try new things. (And you just know the TSA will enjoy your shame too much if you make a mistake.) Pack light, breathe in some of that purple haze, and make the most of your time away with suggestions from other dope explorers.

"Has anybody else heard about this being the greenest Olympics games yet? They say it's because of the recycling programs, but come on, this is British Columbia, Canada. We know the real reason it's the greenest Olympics. It's the B.C. bud."

—MICK FROM *BAKED POTATOES*

"We don't sell or anything like that. If anything, we're probably going to get more tourists who need to know the rules of Vancouver, who might be misled into thinking that it's legal here and stuff like that. That happens a lot."

—VANCOUVER SEED BANK OWNER REBECCA AMBROSE

"I grew up in Vancouver, which has the best weed in the world and good alcohol. You can score just walking down the street, so I did."

—MICHAEL BUBLÉ

"And it was in Vancouver at a nightclub called the Shanghai Junk, located in the heart of Chinatown, where the historic meeting of Cheech and Chong took place."

—TOMMY CHONG, *CHEECH AND CHONG: THE UNAUTHORIZED AUTOBIOGRAPHY*

"We're in Canada and the hydroponic stuff up here is just thorough!"

—EDWARD NORTON

"Nine out of ten people in Jamaica smoke herb. Everyone an outlaw."

—PETER TOSH

"There is one country that is not developing some horrible weapon of destruction, that does not have a secret weapons lab up in the mountains: Jamaica. Irie, mon, Jamaica would never make an atomic bomb. They may make an atomic bong. But I'd rather fight a war with the atomic bong 'cause when the atomic bomb goes off there's devastation and radiation. When the atomic bong goes off, there's celebration!"

—ROBIN WILLIAMS IN *ROBIN WILLIAMS: LIVE ON BROADWAY*

"Sorry to kill the suspense, fellas, but I already know you're going to thoroughly search every inch of not only my stuff, but every inch of me as well. You haven't failed once in the last 15 times I've flown. And yes, I'm well, well aware that the last two stamps on my passport are from Jamaica and Holland, and that I'm currently wearing a 'Pot is good for children and other living things' shirt. Yes, I dressed myself."

—"VAPORELLA" OF *HIGH TIMES*

"Well, the only problem with going to Jamaica to get high is that you might get murdered."

—*WEED: 420 THINGS YOU DIDN'T KNOW OR REMEMBER ABOUT CANNABIS*

"Jamaican Air: Every flight is the red-eye!"

—MITCH HEDBERG

"I hate people who think it's clever to take drugs . . . like customs officers."

—JACK DEE

"We used to go to the movies and sit in the balcony, smoking up a storm. Only a few people would turn around and look for a moment. It was fun, we would laugh."

—TRUMAN CAPOTE, *CONVERSATIONS WITH CAPOTE*

"Herb is all over America, mon. You don't have to bring no herb here anymore."

—PETER TOSH

"What Iowa is to corn, what Kansas is to wheat, the Emerald Triangle is to marijuana."

—TRISH REGAN, HOST, *MARIJUANA INC: INSIDE AMERICA'S POT INDUSTRY*

"I went to my first Phish show. I loved it. . . . I realized, if you don't like a Phish song, you are fucked for the next 45–50 minutes. What do you do? I guess I could go to the post office and mail a certified letter."

—MARGARET CHO

"I think that marijuana should not only be legal, I think it should be a cottage industry. It would be wonderful for the state of Maine. There's some pretty good homegrown dope. I'm sure it would be even better if you could grow it with fertilizers and have greenhouses."

—STEPHEN KING

"I never trust anything in the desert. Spiders, coyotes, cacti, mirages—they're all out there. Waiting for me. I wasn't ever planning on partying out there, but they claimed Burning Man wasn't just any party: It's a festival—one that would apparently change my life."

—NATASHA LEWIN, *HIGH TIMES*

"We want Mendocino to be the Napa of cannabis. Tasting rooms, cannabiseries—like a winery."

—MATT COHEN, GROWER

"I was down in Acapulco, and [Jack Nicholson] said, 'You're drinking too much,' and he was right. So he said, 'Smoke this stuff,' and I did, and it opened me up to a lot of things."

—LARRY HAGMAN

POT SPOTS: EMERALD TRIANGLE
These three counties in Northern Cali (Humboldt, Trinity, and Mendocino) are the biggest pot-producing counties not only in California but in the United States. Though most of the pot farms are blocked by narc-repelling mountains and other types of green, there's a good chance if you run into anyone there, you'll be at most, two degrees from smoking trees.

"San Francisco's so crazy that even the fish are stoned in San Francisco Bay . . . because there's such a level of pot usage in the city, and the waste, even though it's treated, apparently some THC is leaching into the bay, and the fish are swimming in it."

—MICHAEL SAVAGE

"The T.V. and news magazines practically advertised San Francisco as a place to get high and get laid."

—R. CRUMB, ILLUSTRATOR

"I got into that whole 'California consciousness.' I saw all the articles in the *Post* magazine and *Life* about people taking marijuana and LSD and going to Golden Gate Park and all that stuff . . . and the Grateful Dead and [the Jefferson Airplane's] 'Surrealistic Pillow,' I mean, I was a victim of the media, just the same as everyone else was . . . and I just went out there."

—GLENN FREY, OF THE EAGLES,
*TO THE LIMIT: THE UNTOLD
STORY OF THE EAGLES*

"More people smoke marijuana in the United States than voted for George Bush."

—KRIST NOVOSELIC

"I hope you kids learned something today, too, about drugs, which are bad. Except for the ones which aren't, like ibuprofen and aspirin. Marijuana is also okay if it's legally prescribed by a doctor in any of the thirteen states where such laws apply: Alaska, California, Colorado, Hawaii, Maine, Michigan, Montana, Nevada, New Mexico, Oregon, Rhode Island, Vermont and Washington. Time for a road trip! [To the audience] Don't you judge me. Half of you are high right now."

—MIKE HENRY AS CLEVELAND
BROWN ON *THE CLEVELAND
SHOW*

"I was in Italy, and then I took a balloon up my ass to Spain."

—JOHN ENNIS AS MARIJUANA
SMUGGLER #2 ON *MR. SHOW
WITH BOB AND DAVID*

"But those audiences in Spain, they were just so stoned. I don't like playing to audiences like that because they just don't do anything. I'm up here with my band and we're working really hard and they are just stoned."

—GRAHAM COXON

POT SPOTS: BARCELONA

Spain is with it. Smoke it in private, grow it in private, and Spain is absolutely okay with it. And so are the laws! You can light one up in any Spanish city, but Barcelona gets the (s)potlight because it has cool festivals and conventions (Hello Spannabis!) and because the city with its Gaudi architecture looks like it was drawn by Dr. Seuss, which makes your whole high so great.

"What I find most interesting about Portugal is that, despite fully decriminalizing drug use about a decade ago, the country has not seen a huge increase in usage among its population, nor has it become a drug tourist destination spot like Amsterdam."

—TRISH REGAN, BROADCAST
JOURNALIST

"What Jefferson was saying was, Hey! You know, we left this England place 'cause it was bogus; so if we don't get some cool rules ourselves—pronto—we'll just be bogus too! Get it?"

—SEAN PENN AS JEFF SPICOLI
IN *FAST TIMES AT RIDGEMONT
HIGH*

"We want to legalize marijuana. But we can't sell it in cafes like in Amsterdam, because we'd get all the unemployed Germans coming here. We don't want foreigners consuming marijuana in public."

—J. X. DOLEŽAL, CZECH AUTHOR

"When we got to the top of the Pyramid I lit up a marijuana cigarette. . . . Sitting up there high and thoughtful I began to see something about Mexican history I'd never find in books."

—JACK KEROUAC, DESOLATION ANGELS

"What forms of cancer induce in time for the Ziggy Marley concert next Saturday in Denver?"

—TREY PARKER AS RANDY MARSH ON SOUTH PARK

"There are actually more pot dispensaries in Denver than there are Starbucks, and an estimated 500 people a day are applying for a medical license to use pot."

—TRISH REGAN, BROADCAST JOURNALIST

POT SPOTS: DENVER
They are so proud to be called "The Mile High City." In 2005, Denver was the first city in the nation to vote to legalize possession of small amounts of pot—which violated state and federal laws, for sure—but it sent out a powerful message that the people wanted their funky skunky, and that it's time for their laws and politicians to represent them. Good old Denver, making our eyes water out of pride for once.

"Texas is OK if you want to settle down and do your own thing quietly, but it's not for outrageous people, and I was always outrageous."

—JANIS JOPLIN

"I've lived here over twenty-five years, I've never seen [Maui Wowie]. . . . True Blood is a local Hawaiian sativa strain. It's possible it is the real Maui Wowie."

—"JOHNNY DOPE," OF THE SUPREME BEANS GROW LAB ON ATTACK OF THE SHOW!

"Kentucky, I think, is an important place because it used to be one of the primary hemp growers in the nation. Once upon a time, hemp was the number one crop in the United States."

—WOODY HARRELSON

POT SPOTS: BONNAROO

Manchester, Tennessee, represent! Sure Dollywood and "Nash Vegas" are fun, but the real stoner pot spot of the Volunteer State only exists for four days a year. Bonnaroo gets bigger every year, and it attracts performers from Marleys to Phish to Margaret Cho. If you happen to be in Tennessee, you may opt for a high hike through the Smoky Mountains too.

"[In New Jersey] we've legalized marijuana recently. Medical marijuana, but the rest will come."

—SUSAN SARANDON

"Festivals like this is real because you get everything. You can see Stevie Wonder. You can see Dave Matthews Band. You never know what this experience is going to be like until you get here and see it for yourself."

—NAS (ON BONNAROO)

"I went to a private, very hippie-like high school in New York City, right on Central Park West. We spent a lot of time in the park. That makes things pretty clear, doesn't it?"

—MATTHEW BRODERICK

"[I live] mainly in Hawaii, on Maui, in this community of mostly organic farmers. We run off solar and wind and generators if necessary. I've been there nine years and it's Shangri La to me. I have lots of fruit and coconut trees, and every day I swim, I surf, climb coconut trees, play with my kids, eat mangoes. There's no form to it, which I kind of like."

—WOODY HARRELSON

"When I lived in the East Village, you had to go to various doors to get the grass, like you'd slip money through the blue door or the black door or the red door, and somebody would hand you this little brown envelope with pot in it."

—SAMANTHA MCEWEN, ARTIST, *KEITH HARING: THE AUTHORIZED BIOGRAPHY*

"My stories about the Big Apple, my reefers keeping me sky-high—wherever I went, I was the life of the party."

—MALCOLM X, *THE AUTOBIOGRAPHY OF MALCOLM X*

FINE FUMES: SOUR D
Sour Diesel is one of the most ubiquitous and potent strains today, and a favorite of East Coast tokers. It's hard to hide this strain's pungent scent, but it may be worth it for the high, which will hit your head like a Mack truck.

"They grow so much of it down at the South Pole it's unbelievable. Those guys were high all the time."

—KEVIN C. MCDEVITT, A NAVY SECURITY GUARD

POT SPOTS: MCMURDO STATION

A pot spot for the most extreme and the most isolated. The cultural scene in Antarctica is pretty bleak. Given little to do after work and access to plenty of indoor agricultural equipment, staffers at this U.S. scientific base have an easy (though risky) time growing and using the ish. It helps them adjust to life on the ice. The station is a pretty sweet setup for the stoner with the right credentials. Maybe it's time to rethink grad school. The previous quote is from the '80s, but fun gardens have been found there very recently. It just doesn't make the papers much.

"It breaks down like this, okay: it's legal to buy it, it's legal to own it, and if you're the proprietor of a hash bar, it's legal to sell it. It's illegal to carry it, but that doesn't matter 'cause—get a load of this, all right—if you get stopped by a cop in Amsterdam, it's illegal for them to search you."

—JOHN TRAVOLTA AS VINCENT,
IN *PULP FICTION*

"I've been traveling a lot, went to Amsterdam. That was really cool. That really opened up my eyes . . . and made them red."

—DAN LEVY, COMEDIAN

"I'm not a massive fan of the 'dam. It used to be pretty laid back and serene in the '80s. It just seems to be full of c***s these days. They all seem to be English and all."

—NOEL GALLAGHER OF OASIS

"When you go to Amsterdam, for example, you go to where the stoners hang out in Amsterdam, you almost never see a fight break out. If you go to the bars of England, Scotland, or Germany, fights break out all the time. In other words, alcohol induces violent behavior. I've never known a stoner, or a pot head, to want to start a fight."

—ERIC BRAEDEN, SOAP STAR

"Today in Amsterdam the charcoal drawing she made of me naked doesn't look as ugly as I felt yesterday. This is the real city of angels. They remade me in their image."

—YOUTH, IN STEW'S *PASSING STRANGE*

CHAPTER 18

WORST-CASE CANNABIS SCENARIOS

"That's when one of the guys pulled out a gun and held it to his head. They were telling him as they put the pipe to his lips, 'Hit that! Hit that, motherfucker! Hit it or I'm gonna kill you!'"

—Jeremy London, actor (quoting his kidnapper)

This book may seem to have a pro-cannabis bias. (Free Marc Emery!) But it's really important that you realize that your life with weed isn't a Candy Land–style path to happiness. Sure, it feels like that way 99.999 percent of the time, but we have to allow for some counterpoint, I'm told. We saw how you can lose a buzz, but it's possible you could lose a lot more.

This isn't reefer madness. This is some straight dope about people who had a really kickass time, and then abruptly didn't.

Was it worth it? Probably. Will they smoke up again? If they survived, absolutely. You gotta chase the highs, amigos. But here is why they and you might think twice.

"Unlike alcohol, when you take too much at one time, you don't pass out. You more than likely run the risk of an unpredictable and unpleasant bummer."

—SONNY BONO, *MARIJUANA* (1968)

"All I could think of was, 'you're gonna be the first guy ever to be fired from a weed movie . . . for being high.'"

—JIM BREUER

"Police in Brooklyn were called after a four-year-old boy showed up at kindergarten with a bag of marijuana in his shoe. The drugs had a reported street value of five milks and a cupcake."

—TINA FEY ON *SATURDAY NIGHT LIVE*

"Stop what? The bong? I don't think it can be stopped, man. . . . It killed all my friends, man, and it almost got me. Well, it got all my brain cells, but that's okay 'cause I wasn't using them anyway."

—TOMMY CHONG AS JIMBO IN *EVIL BONG*

"I know personally now, that it was a very dangerous thing to do. In difficult situations, say at night, if anyone moved near me I might have taken a shot at him."

—JACKIE ROBINSON SR., *I NEVER HAD IT MADE* (ON COMBINING WAR AND WEED)

"You have smoked yourself retarded."

—DAVE CHAPPELLE AS THURGOOD JENKINS IN *HALF BAKED*

"I think I may be having sort of a . . . a mini freak-out here. Just tell me I don't have to stay in this room."

—SETH MACFARLANE AS QUAGMIRE (C-3PO) ON *FAMILY GUY*

"It is, like, the best medicine. Because it fixes everything. Jonah broke his elbow once. He just got high, and it still clicks, but, I mean, he's okay."

—SETH ROGEN AS BEN IN *KNOCKED UP*

"It's like the one time I smoked pot. I didn't wanna do it in the first place. I had a horrible time. Then Ronny Templeton's brother called the police and we got arrested. The one time I ever did anything illegal."

—MEG RYAN AS KATE IN *FRENCH KISS*

"A fourteen-year-old Indiana girl was arrested after she came to a middle school with a handgun, ammunition, and six small bags of marijuana. Man, Dakota Fanning's growing up so fast!"

—AMY POEHLER ON *SATURDAY NIGHT LIVE*

"Did Doogie Howser just steal my fucking car?"

—JOHN CHO AS *HAROLD IN HAROLD AND KUMAR GO TO WHITE CASTLE*

"I don't smoke much pot anymore. One of the last times I was stoned, I was convinced that I would die unless I kept moving my body. So I sat there, baked, waving my arms around like a crazy person."

—SETH MACFARLANE

"As I looked into the bowl, and followed the pattern around, I fell through the bottom of the bowl, where the pattern wasn't complete. It was like a hole in the bottom of a basket, and I just fell on out. I fell out into nowhere, and nothing. . . ."

—STEPHEN GASKIN, *AMAZING DOPE TALES*

"My grandma drank all my pot!"

—ALLEN COVERT AS ALEX IN *GRANDMA'S BOY*

"Danbury wasn't a prison, it was a crime school. I went in with a bachelor of marijuana, came out with a doctorate of cocaine."

—JOHNNY DEPP AS GEORGE IN
BLOW

"I remembered reading on the Internet that if I smoked 1,256 bong rips, the amount of THC would be enough to kill me. Then I set to work."

—JENN SHAGRIN AS MARY JANE
IN DESPERATE HIPPIES (A LOW-
BUDGET, INDEPENDENT PARODY
FILM)

HIGH CREDENTIALS: "DUSTIN MICHAELS"

This sidebar is a sad one. Michaels was a porn model/actor who lost his life to weed. Actually, it looks like he lost his life to trying to swallow his weed to hide it from cops, being Tasered, and then choking on his weed. Sometimes you make stupid decisions on weed (or on alcohol, or when you're tired, or scared of the po-po), but do we really need to live in a world where you face a choice between swallowing a stash and being arrested? Remember him. It's a sad loss for all of us, especially for straight women and gay dudes . . . also his friends and family.

"We overheard the guys saying, 'Hey, we're going to arrest Cheech and Chong.' The cops were talking amongst themselves and they were arguing about who was going to take us down because they were all our biggest fans."

—TOMMY CHONG

"You're just like me. You get up in the morning and smoke weed. You obsess about the Jamaican man across the hall."

—CARRIE FISHER AS ROSEMARY
TO LIZ LEMON ON 30 ROCK

"We got arrested for a misdemeanor amount of [marijuana]—we didn't have no pound. The police just found something minor in a garbage can the dog sniffed."

—BRYAN "BABY" WILLIAMS,
AKA BIRDMAN

"Woodstock turned out to be a disaster. Everybody was stuck in the mud and people got sick."

—JOHNNY RIVERS

"I used to sell weed, and was kicked out of music and art for that."

—KURTIS BLOW, RAPPER

"One time a producer and artist got me so stoned I had to get up and take a walk around the block to get my head on straight. We started early that afternoon and didn't finish until well after dawn the next day. Heck, if they were willing to pay me all that overtime. . . ."

—JOE OSBORN

"I'm gonna go call 911. What's the number? . . . There is something wrong with my friend. I think he smoked some nutmeg or something."

—SETH GREEN AS MICK IN IDLE HANDS

Colonel (Claude Piéplu): Marijuana isn't a drug. Look at what goes on in Vietnam. From the general down to the private, they all smoke.

Mme. Thevenot (Delphine Seyrig): As a result, once a week they bomb their own troops.

Colonel: If they bomb their own troops, they must have their reasons.

—THE DISCREET CHARM OF THE BOURGEOISIE

"Maybe you're the infertile one around here. Maybe every time you smoke a little doobie, you're killing our unborn children."

—JENNIFER ANISTON AS JUSTINE IN THE GOOD GIRL

"Um, yeah, on a list of bad ideas, that one goes, way up there. 'Oh, police officers, please, as you inspect a crime scene, which is now our van, please, ignore the colorful piñata, filled with marijuana, in case you happen to come across it, because it played no part, you know, whatsoever in the demise of this unfortunate, young, woman.'"

—JONATHAN TUCKER AS MORGAN IN THE TEXAS CHAINSAW MASSACRE (2003)

"This is sort of an unusual question, but do you have any marijuana I might be able to buy from you? Our car exploded last night and I'm practically all out of my own."

—PAULO COSTANZO AS RUBIN IN
ROAD TRIP

"This chip-off-the-old-bong is our son Harley. If he had an Indian name, it would be 'Busted Condom.'"

—BRYAN CRANSTON AS WOODROW SNIDER IN THANKSGIVING FAMILY REUNION

"When Paul was arrested in Japan for having hash in his luggage, I thought he'd be out that night. But it became really serious stuff when he was kept in a cell. I became more fearful as the days went by. . . . They would not give him a pencil to write, in case he poked his eyes out, or a guitar, because they feared he might hang himself with the strings."

—LINDA MCCARTNEY

"I can take pot or leave it. I got busted in Japan for it. I was nine days without it and there wasn't a hint of withdrawal, nothing."

—PAUL MCCARTNEY

FINE FUMES: HASHISH

A killer of buzzes will say hash isn't pot. It's close enough. It is made of compressed cannabis trichomes, and has the same effect—only more intense because it's got a higher concentration of the good shit. And it looks a little like shit, but you'll happily eat it.

"The euphoria was soon replaced with panic as the drug refused to wear off. I found myself in the bathroom pissing out what was left of it. And as I stared at the bubbles I was making in the bowl, they slowly transformed into the head of Abraham Lincoln as he appears on the penny."

—LEWIS BLACK,
NOTHING'S SACRED

"In 1965, I'd signed a contract for *The Sons of Katie Elder* with John Wayne, but a week before shooting I went to a Hollywood party that the vice squad busted because of marijuana. I was hand-cuffed and photos of me got in the papers with headlines like 'Ex-Disney Child Star Arrested for Pot!' So Wayne and the producers fired me."

—TOMMY KIRK

"Okay, here's the game plan. Flush the drugs, throw the gun in the river, we'll tell everyone it was exhaustion."

—JENNIFER COOLIDGE AS
BOBBIE ON *JOEY*

"One day there was a SWAT team outside, and everybody broke my doors down and hog-tied me in my own living room."

—JASON HARRIS OF JEROME
BAKER DESIGNS ON *ATTACK OF
THE SHOW!*

"You guys are the biggest fuck-ups in the history of dope dealing. That's a huge fuckin' statement."

—BILLY BOB THORNTON AS JACK
MARSDEN IN *HOMEGROWN*

HIGH CREDENTIALS: JASON HARRIS

Known for his Jerome Baker Designs, Harris blew and assembled some of the most artful bongs known to stonerkind. After his DEA arrest, the value of his unsold pieces shot up in value. You could be seeing four figures for a medium-sized pipe, and maybe it's worth it to have such undeniable stoner cred.

> "I am so stoned. Stop being stoned, Mary. I don't want him to see me stoned!"
>
> —KIRSTEN DUNST AS MARY IN *ETERNAL SUNSHINE OF THE SPOTLESS MIND*

> "You cannot pass out around white people. Every time white dudes pass out around each other they always do some borderline gay shit when the guy's asleep."
>
> —DAVE CHAPPELLE

> "My mother told me that she had to go into town to buy some marijuana. She sat at the mirror and wound a black scarf around her head. My mother stared at the mirror and took great care to wind the scarf properly. She rode down the hill on her bicycle: 'I won't be long.' By the time she left it was the start of the afternoon . . . and the hottest day of the year."
>
> —ARI DELON, *PLEASE KILL ME: THE UNCENSORED ORAL HISTORY OF PUNK* (ON WARHOL SUPERSTAR NICO'S FATAL BIKE RIDE)

> "I was just sitting there doing my normal routine, and I guess someone thought I looked suspicious and called the cops. They found an old pipe that had some residue on it or something."
>
> —TOMMY MORRISON, FORMER HEAVYWEIGHT CHAMP

"[One of] the guys who was there looking around said, 'Sorry, I can see you smoke weed, but we have this butter [containing cannabis resin] here, which is instant manufacturing and instant imprisonment.'"

—JOHN "AXE" AKURANGI, FOR-
MER RUGBY PLAYER

"I was with the wife, ordered some room service and was butt naked. Next thing rozzers are at the door so I pulled me kecks on and next thing they are rooting through our cases. They took my herb and were dead happy because it was the first famous person they had arrested."

—JON MCCLURE, REVEREND
AND THE MAKERS FRONT MAN

"On the way home from the studio we were really stoned—we were driving through the woods and got lost and kept on seeing body parts of human bodies along the road. Like an arm here, and a head there. Everybody saw it. We were glad to get back to New York after that."

—DEE DEE RAMONE, PLEASE
KILL ME: THE UNCENSORED
ORAL HISTORY OF PUNK

"Panic hit me, I don't know why. Yes I do: I was stoned. Each face in the shop seemed to wear a spectral grin of greed and sick pleasure."

—KEVIN KILLIAN, POET AND
AUTHOR, BEDROOMS HAVE
WINDOWS

"He was stoned all the time, which made him less than the most efficient road manager. I got tired of it. Getting stoned was the band's job."

—DON HENLEY, TO THE LIMIT:
THE UNTOLD STORY OF THE
EAGLES

"Someone was talking through my mouth."

—JOHN MALKOVICH IN BEING
JOHN MALKOVICH

"We should go home. I don't think we should be out in the world like this. . . . I don't remember how to drive!"

—BRIAN POSEHN AS BRIAN
ON THE SARAH SILVERMAN
PROGRAM

"Myself, I'm a pothead. It's no secret. Everyone knows that. I go on the road and forget everything else. I could have easily just written them a check for whatever amount, but no . . . I waited until they knocked on the door and were like, 'We got your truck and we outta here.'"

—METHOD MAN (ACCUSING WEED OF MAKING HIM FORGET TO PAY TAXES)

"What the hell are we drug testing a janitor for? What's the worst he gonna do? Drop the mop? If you're thirty-nine years old and a janitor you should get to smoke a joint."

—D. L. HUGHLEY

CHAPTER 19

ONCE UPON A TIME WHEN I WAS HIGH

"From now on, I smoke weed exclusively with white people. . . . All white people talk about when they get high is other times when they got high. I could listen to that shit all night."

—Dave Chappelle

High School may not have been like Ridgemont or Shermer High (from *The Breakfast Club*), but you probably had some really, really great highs anyway.

Some moments in life seem like a stoned fairytale, where all of those things we smoke to forget actually slip away. They make the stories that end with laughter and "Dude, no way!"

What makes the stoner way of life better than any other? Let's take a trip down Memory Lane and find out!

"Millions of new thoughts fucking flooding in my brain. It's like I was ripping down walls and shit was flowing in, like, wow!"

—Joe Rogan

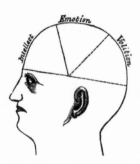

"I can remember another early visual experience with cannabis, in which I viewed a candle flame and discovered in the heart of the flame, standing with magnificent indifference, the black-hatted and -cloaked Spanish gentleman who appears on the label of the Sandeman sherry bottle. Looking at fires when high, by the way, especially through one of those prism kaleidoscopes which image their surroundings, is an extraordinarily moving and beautiful experience."

—Carl Sagan

"I'll give you a little hint on that *Punk'd* thing. That was back in my first-album creative days. That's why I looked the way I did, if that makes any sense to you. . . . That was a trippy experience. That was why I was completely glassy-eyed. As a matter of fact, I was like, okay, I got to stop doing this. I don't do that anymore!"

—Justin Timberlake

"'I get much more involved in ordinary tasks than when I'm straight; they're completely absorbing' is a very common effect."

—Charles T. Tart, PhD, *On Being Stoned*

"Hitting a tennis ball is easier on marijuana because the pot slows everything down and that includes the ball. It will seem to float your way when returned, hang in space and invite you to smack it a good one. Of course, the pot will also slow up your own movement and put you in a slow motion mode as you go for the ball, but that just makes things more interesting."

—EVAN KELIHER, *GRANDPA'S MARIJUANA HANDBOOK*

"I've waited all my life to say this, Bob: '420.'"

—STONER EVAN GODING (BIDDING ON *THE PRICE IS RIGHT*)

"I owe a lot of the good ideas I've ever had in my life to pot."

—BILL MAHER

"[John] Belushi was the first person to show me how to roll a joint. It was very exciting. You would come to the seventeenth floor [of 30 Rock], and as you walked down the hall, the stench of marijuana would greet you like about a hundred feet away from the offices."

—*SATURDAY NIGHT LIVE* WRITER TOM SCHILLER, *LIVE FROM NEW YORK: AN UNCENSORED HISTORY OF SATURDAY NIGHT LIVE*

"The Beatles thing had just gone beyond comprehension. We were smoking marijuana for breakfast. We were well into marijuana and nobody could communicate with us, because we were just all glazed eyes, giggling all the time."

—JOHN LENNON

"One thing he did introduce us to was pot. . . . Bob came round to our hotel, and he said to us, 'Here, try a bit of this.' It is very indiscreet to say this, because I don't know whether Bob is telling people he turned The Beatles on to marijuana. But it was funny."

—PAUL McCARTNEY, *THE BEATLES ANTHOLOGY*

"Bob Dylan had heard one of our records where we said, 'I can't hide,' and he had understood, 'I get high.' He came running and said to us, 'Right, guys, I've got some really good grass.' How could you not dig a bloke like that?"

—JOHN LENNON, THE BEATLES ANTHOLOGY

"In a recent interview, Paul McCartney confessed that Bob Dylan turned the Beatles on to marijuana. In return, George Harrison turned Dylan on to looking old and haggard."

—NORM MACDONALD ON SATURDAY NIGHT LIVE

"We came out of the studio after ten days, with twelve songs, and just hung out and talked and had the basketball game on in the background. . . . We smoked some weed and just chilled and the album was done, man. That's what it's supposed to be, man—an exchange of energy, an exchange of ideas, just sittin' back and enjoying yourself, man."

—DJ MUGGS FROM CYPRESS HILL

HIGH CREDENTIALS: DJ MUGGS

Muggs is the DJ and producer of the hip-hop/rap metal/blanket-urban group Cypress Hill. He stands out in the group as first-place stoner due to an incident where he lit up while performing on *Saturday Night Live*. Apparently that gets you banned from the show, but it will also get you a permanent home in the iTunes libraries of weed lovers everywhere.

"I had come to feel that there was more to living than science, a time of awakening of my social consciousness and amiability, a time when I was open to new experiences."

—CARL SAGAN

"The world became even more wonderful, my limbs felt as if they were made of rubber and, catching sight of myself in the mirror, I gazed, without self-consciousness, for perhaps five minutes, into my own eyes."

—JOE ORTON, THE ORTON DIARIES

"The pot was sticky with lots of buds, and its smell reminded me of a Christmas tree, though not the one perched atop the barstool."

—DAVID SEDARIS, *WHEN YOU ARE ENGULFED IN FLAMES*

"Sometimes it helps us take journeys into deep and wonderful places and embrace the passionate memories of our past when we're stoned."

—KEVIN SMITH, *SMODCAST*

"I've been around it. In fact, we met Hillary [Clinton]. She came in Willie's bus . . . and I think she inhaled."

—MERLE HAGGARD

"Once I was on a ship, with 43 crew, none of whom smoked, and we were away from England for like 7 or 8 months and by the time we came back over half the crew were turned on and I had the captain's permission to smoke."

—RICHARD NEVILLE, *PLAY POWER*

"Yes, Dustin Diamond from *Saved by the Bell* had to roll down Melrose Avenue and shake down a dealer for his bag of weed."

—DUSTIN DIAMOND,
BEHIND THE BELL

"It was actually in Chicago when I first picked up my first stick of gage. . . . And I'm telling you, I had myself a ball. . . . That's why it really puzzles me to see marijuana connected with narcotics—dope and all that kind of crap."

—LOUIS ARMSTRONG

"I think anyone who ignores what they learn while high is walking in the dark jungle without a flashlight."

—STEPHEN GASKIN,
AMAZING DOPE TALES

"After my mother found the pot, she came to me and said, 'Dear, I thought instead of you going outside and smoking pot where you might get caught and get in trouble—I thought you and I might experiment with it together.'"

—CARRIE FISHER, WISHFUL
DRINKING (ON MOM, DEBBIE
REYNOLDS)

"What a night! I was in more laps than a napkin."

—AMY SPANGER AS SALLY IN
REEFER MADNESS: THE MOVIE
MUSICAL

"I'm beginnin' to think I liked you a lot better when you used to smoke all that reefer and we'd fuck in your Pinto."

—BILLY BOB THORNTON AS
SHERIFF DARL HARDWICK IN
THE BADGE

"Oh, yes, there was Mexican shit back there in the early Sixties that was so strong . . . that would put Vikings in your oatmeal and jewels shining in the wall if you smoked it!"

—WAVY GRAVY, PEACE ACTIVIST
AND WOODSTOCK EMCEE, *CAN'T
FIND MY WAY HOME*

"Remember, we were young. Spring break, sophomore year, I got high in my bedroom, and my parents walked in and smelled it, and so I told them that you had gotten stoned and then jumped out the window."

—DAVID SCHWIMMER AS ROSS
ON *FRIENDS*

"We was stuck on those steps for hours just laughing. I was like, 'Dude, I'm seeing purple stuff!' Like actually, you know what I'm sayin'? We was gone. And from that time on, I was like, 'Man, this is my new thing.'"

—KRAYZIE BONE

"It was an insanely huge party, and I just got back, and . . . I may have partied too much, but you know I have to fly drugged. So, I'm still slightly drugged, and I'm sure somewhere in me, I'm still partying."

—WHOOPI GOLDBERG

"A common experience is 'I can get so wound up in thoughts or fantasies that I won't notice what's going on around me or won't hear someone talking to me unless they attract my attention forcibly.'"

—CHARLES T. TART, PHD, *ON
BEING STONED*

"One's condition on marijuana is always existential. One can feel the importance of each moment and how it is changing one. One feels one's being, one becomes aware of the enormous apparatus of nothingness—the hum of a hi-fi set, the emptiness of a pointless interruption, one becomes aware of the war between each of us, how the nothingness in each of us seeks to attack the being of others, how our being in turn is attacked by the nothingness in others."

—NORMAN MAILER, *CONVERSA-
TIONS WITH NORMAN MAILER*

"Every once in a while, when there weren't other projects or on Friday afternoons when the whole crew got stoned and drank beer and were therefore reluctant to operate power tools, everybody would come down to the cellar and we'd have a shoveling party."

—DAVID GESSNER,
SICK OF NATURE

"I went down by the sewage treatment plant by the Loop, where the river is entirely industrialized. It's all concrete banks and effluvia by the Marina Towers. So I smoked this joint and then it hit me. I thought, 'What you gotta do is play your own simple blues.'"

—IGGY POP, PLEASE KILL ME:
THE UNCENSORED ORAL HISTORY OF PUNK

"I started to laugh hysterically at just about everything that was said, and with a real side splitting kind of laugh which I hadn't laughed in a long time!"

—D. CHRISTOPHER TOTTEN,
AUTOBIOGRAPHY OF A HIPPIE

"I had never taken it before, and was instructed by a boisterous young poet, whose English was no better than my French. He gave me a little pellet, if I am not forgetting, an hour before dinner, and another after we had dined together at some restaurant. As we were going through the streets to the meeting-place of the Martinists, I felt suddenly that a cloud I was looking at floated in an immense space, and for an instant my being rushed out, as it seemed, into that space with ecstasy."

—WILLIAM BUTLER YEATS

"I learned how to swim because of Iggy [Pop]. . . . He would get stoned and almost certainly fall into the pool, and be floating there, face down."

—LEEE CHILDERS, MANAGER OF
BOWIE, SID VICIOUS, AND OTHERS,
PLEASE KILL ME: THE UNCENSORED ORAL HISTORY OF PUNK

"The first time I got stoned I was a freshman in college. One bong hit filled up my lungs like a three-alarm fire, and I could not think straight for at least a day or two."

—ELIZABETH WURTZEL, MORE,
NOW, AGAIN

"The first time . . . it was in eighth grade. I think we smoked it out of an apple in my friend's backyard, and then went to an eighth-grade dance and had a pretty good time."

—JAMES FRANCO

"A specific question dealing with marijuana experiences was 'I feel so aware of what people are thinking that it must be telepathy, mind reading, rather than just being more sensitive to the subtle cues in the behavior.' This was a fairly frequent occurrence."

—CHARLES T. TART, PHD, ON BEING STONED

"I've often felt telepathic and receptive to inexplicable messages my whole life. I can stave those off when I'm not high. When I'm high—well, they come in and there's less of a veil, so to speak. So if ever I need some clarity, or a quantum leap in my own consciousness, or a quantum leap in terms of writing something or getting an answer, it's a quick way for me to get it."

—ALANIS MORISSETTE

"I was like, 'Man, I get to smoke with Cheech!' It's almost like if Elvis Presley said, 'Get a guitar, man, let's play.' So I smoked some . . . and it took me forty-five minutes to back out of the driveway."

—GEORGE LOPEZ ON LOPEZ TONIGHT

"I do remember having this sensation that I was being picked up by my ears."

—EDWARD NORTON

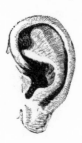

"When drugs came around I sampled them just like anybody else but I never became dependent creatively on drugs; like various cartoonists in the underground never did anything if they weren't stoned. That was the prerequisite for sitting down and drawing."

—BILL GRIFFITH

"[Sly Stone's] home studio was a nice place to hang my head. Everybody was on marijuana and coke. Sly would stay up all night, and just play, play, play. One time I came in, and he was laying on the piano asleep. I woke him up, and he looked at me, and started singing."

—BOBBY WOMACK

"Twas the night before a party, when all through the town, no pigs were stirring, no cops were around. We drank Seagram's, and smoked Panama Reds, while visions of the munchies danced through our heads."

—THORA BIRCH AS LINCOLN ROTH IN *THE SMOKERS*

"Mick, Pnub, I'll never forget all those times we sat around, watched TV and got really, really stoned. And all those other times we just . . . well I guess that's all we did."

—DEVON SAWA AS ANTON IN *IDLE HANDS*

POT SPOTS: HONEYSUCKLE ROSE IV

Also known as Willie Nelson's chauffeured hotbox, this tour bus is his home on the road. If you manage to get invited onboard, sample his stash, and with permission, sign his guitar, Trigger, well then, my friend, you have scored the ultimate stoner hat trick, and you reign supreme.

"Whenever there was a hot Playmate in the room, I would always have a good time. It brought more life to the party. I would be belligerent and act like a total fool, but the girl and I would usually mess around, smoke some weed, and kiss a little. That was fun."

—KENDRA WILKINSON,
SLIDING INTO HOME

"[Allen] Ginsberg clearly thought he was coming back to Brad's apartment to get laid. But Brad had no idea who he was, that he had dragged Walt Whitman home. He treated the whole encounter like some big joke. Eventually we all wound up sitting on the floor in our living room, chanting and smoking pot, and listening to Ginsberg read his poetry."

—SUSAN BLUESTEIN DAVIS,
*AFTER MIDNIGHT: THE LIFE AND
DEATH OF BRAD DAVIS*

"It makes you lie around on the floor and look at the ceiling. What's wrong with that?"

—BILLY BOB THORNTON

"My teacher, Linda, was my enabler. She believed in me so she left me alone and let me do what I wanted when I wanted. She even let me come and go and would cover for me when I was too stoned to go to the next class. She was a stoner's dream."

—JOE ANDOE, ARTIST, *JUBILEE
CITY: A MEMOIR AT FULL SPEED*

"In exchange for free dope, Willow would give me free records. We'd smoke the dope and listen to the records while having sex at my apartment. Not a terrible arrangement, all things considered. It was Willow, after all, who gave me my first AC/DC album."

—DAVE MUSTAINE OF MEGA-
DETH, *MUSTAINE: A HEAVY
METAL MEMOIR*

"I would like to be president someday, so no, I have not smoked marijuana. I ate a brownie once, at a party in college. It was intense. It was kind of indescribable, actually. I felt like I was floating. Turns out there wasn't actually any pot in the brownie. It was just an insanely good brownie."

—AMY POEHLER AS LES-
LIE KNOPE ON *PARKS AND
RECREATION*

"As usual, marijuana saves an otherwise disastrous day."

—ELDEN HENSON AS PNUB IN
IDLE HANDS

"The first time I officially got high? Thirteen. That was an event. I was in Staten Island, at a friend of mine's house, and his name was Blunt, of all people. And the way he taught me how to get high—and I've been doing this to people who don't know how to get high ever since—he said he would give me a shotgun and told me to just breathe in slow, and that's what I did. I ain't looked back since, straight up."

—METHOD MAN

"We'd smoke weed in rolled-up old newspapers, stinking up the bus with these fat joints until everyone was coughing and falling out."

—ETTA JAMES, *RAGE TO
SURVIVE*

"I don't know if it was the whole audi-ence getting stoned out of their minds getting ready for the Floyd thing or what it was, but it was like playing to a painting."

—LES CLAYPOOL, GUITARIST OF PRIMUS

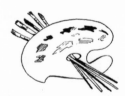

CHAPTER 20

YOU MUST HAVE BEEN HIGH WHEN YOU . . .

"To this day, I am puzzled about exactly what happened at the Miami International Airport. . . ."
—Dionne Warwick

We do a lot of crazy shit when we're high. We eat too much—maybe an entire jar of pickles, probably everything on the Value Menu at Wendy's. Sometimes we think our friends are out to get us. Then there's that time you worked at Subway and couldn't remember how to make a turkey melt. And remember when you thought you died?

We owe our greatest moments to our wacky weed. No need to be embarrassed—shit happens. Now take a few more hits and read on to see how other potheads have made the most of their high times.

"I was invited to participate in part because I had been cleared to use medical marijuana legally last year by a gynecologist who said he knew nothing about back trouble but believed cannabis might just be the best cure for my pain."

—STEVE LOPEZ, *L.A. TIMES* COL-
UMNIST (WORKING WITH COPS TO
TEST OUT STONED DRIVING)

"We are multitasking pot smok-ers. We also can do several things at once. Just the other day, for example, Doug was (1) walking down the street, (2) talking on his cell phone, (3) putting eye drops in his eyes, and (4) getting hit by a car."

—DOUG BENSON, ARJ BARKER,
AND TONY CAMIN, *THE
MARIJUANA-LOGUES: EVERY-
THING ABOUT POT THAT WE
COULD REMEMBER*

"[Ashton Kutcher] told me this later because I don't even remem-ber seeing him that night, but later he called me and said I just said one thing to him over and over again . . . I just said, 'I love you. You're my brother.'"

—TOPHER GRACE (ON FIRST
TIME STONED)

"I hang out a lot with these Rus-sian clowns. They speak very little English, and I speak no Russian, but we get along swim-mingly, using very few words."

—JOSEPH GORDON-LEVITT

"I think more research could be use-ful. Dude, I didn't even get a chance to dip into my bag of Skywalker."

—STEVE LOPEZ, *L.A. TIMES* COL-
UMNIST (ON HIS EXPERIMENT)

"In answer to the question, 'What was the Magna Carta?' you wrote 'Planet Zoot.' And in response to the query, 'What was the capital of France during the Nazi occupation?' you traced your hand."

—STEPHEN COLBERT AS MR. NOBLET ON *STRANGERS WITH CANDY*

Dean Cain (Obba Babatundé): What on earth are you wearing?
   Tuan (Trieu Tran): BUFU.
   Dean Cain: BUFU?
   Tuan: By us. Fuck you!

—*HOW HIGH*

"Some people say that if you smoke pot for a long time, it'll affect your ability to reason with maturity. People who say that are poo poo ca ca pee pee faces."

—DOUG BENSON, ARJ BARKER, AND TONY CAMIN, *THE MARIJUANA-LOGUES: EVERYTHING ABOUT POT THAT WE COULD REMEMBER*

"Every year Oscar attempts the 420 mile walk from Newport Beach to Berkeley, California. In the twelve years he's attempted this, he's never made it past U.C. Irvine."

—RON HOWARD AS THE NARRATOR ON *ARRESTED DEVELOPMENT*

"Carrots. Medicinal carrots. Personal-use medicinal carrots that were here when I moved in. And I'm holding it for a friend."

—ALAN TUDYK AS ALPHA/ KEPLER ON *DOLLHOUSE*

"The '60s ain't over 'til the fat lady gets high."

—JERRY GARCIA (ATTRIBUTED FREQUENTLY TO KEN KESEY)

"Mom, Dad, the drugs are more important than you!"

—DENISE GALIK AS LISA IN *DON'T ANSWER THE PHONE*

"I got so stoned that during dinner I became convinced that a diminutive DJ called Speedy, who was also on the press trip for a regional radio station, was trying to kill me."

—Tom Sykes, journalist, What Did I Do Last Night?

Richard Vernon (Paul Gleason): What if your dope was on fire?

John Bender (Judd Nelson): Impossible, sir . . . it's in Johnson's underwear.

—The Breakfast Club

Man Stoner (Tommy Chong): It's mostly Maui Wowie, man, but it's got some Labrador in it.

Pedro (Cheech Marin): What's Labrador?

Man Stoner: It's dog shit.

Pedro: What?

Man Stoner: Yeah my dog ate my stash, man. Had it on the table, and the little motherfucker ate it, man. So I had to follow him around with a little baggie for three days before I got it back. Really blew the dog's mind.

Pedro: You mean we're smoking dog shit, man?

—Up in Smoke

"Quentin came to visit with the script. We talked about the backstory and about movies. I got up the next day and there were five empty bottles of wine lying on the floor—five—and something resembling smoking apparatus. I don't know what that was about. Somehow I had agreed to do the movie, and six weeks later I was in a uniform playing Aldo Raine."

—Brad Pitt on being cast in Inglourious Basterds

"You know, I never thought I'd say this to anybody, but you smoke entirely too much reefer."

—DAVE CHAPPELLE AS THURGOOD JENKINS IN *HALF BAKED*

"My humor came from seeing my parents have sex, smoke weed, my mom being naked—just weird hippie stuff, twisted R-rated humor. . . ."

—SHIA LABEOUF

"We smoked a joint and congratulated ourselves on the decision to carry dope into India—there had been no customs at all."

—TOM DAVIS, *THIRTY-NINE YEARS OF SHORT-TERM MEMORY LOSS*

"By the time we got to Florida, we were high. At the hotel . . . everybody ran into their rooms and then jumped into the swimming pool. We didn't have a show that night. I jumped in with my drawers on and messed around, and pulled my arm out of the socket. . . . I told the guy I fell in the tub."

—TIGER MARTIN, *THE GREAT DRUMMERS OF R&B FUNK & SOUL*

"One time, my group the Upright Citizen's Brigade got to host the Cannabis Cup in Amsterdam. I don't remember much of it."

—AMY POEHLER

"A couple of brown plants on the edges of some of those (forests) did catch on fire. But a section of soldiers that was downwind from that had some ill effects and decided that was probably not the right course of action."

—GENERAL RICK HILLIER, CHIEF OF THE DEFENSE STAFF OF THE CANADIAN FORCES

FINE FUMES: TANGERINE DREAM

This sunset-tinged strain got pot-dom's finest honor in 2010, taking the *High Times* Cannabis Cup. It's said to smell and taste like tangerines. What magic is this? Regardless, it's the high that counts, and in the end, the citrussy notes won over weed's toughest (though still way relaxed) connoisseurs.

"Hi, I'm Snoop Dogg, and we're selling brownies to help out my football league, so the kids can get helmets."

—SNOOP DOGG ON *LOPEZ TONIGHT* (A SKETCH)

"Restless, and in desperate need of adventure, I quit my job at an insurance company to travel west with a couple of guys I smoked pot with, scandalizing my family."

—MINK STOLE

"Last time I smoked that stuff they found me on top of the Sears tower trying to build a nest."

—ROBIN WILLIAMS AS JACK IN
CLUB PARADISE

Jane (Anna Faris): It's really bright out, officer.
Officer Jones (Michael Shamus Wiles): Would you mind removing your hand from your forehead?
Jane: It's really bright out.

—SMILEY FACE

"Oops. Turns out I'd forgotten to put cheese on some of the pizzas. The customer and my manager were equally unhappy. As you can expect, I was still in a good mood."

—KENDRA WILKINSON, SLIDING INTO HOME (ON WORKING AT PAPA JOHN'S)

"I was in Florida with Burt Stern, the photographer who shot Marilyn Monroe on the beach with a sweater, and we smoked a joint. The bathing suit kept coming off in the water, and I just ripped it off. I was very comfortable being naked."

—ROSANNA ARQUETTE

"I'd come to work, loud and wild and half-high on liquor or reefers, and I'd stay that way, jamming sandwiches at people until we got to New York."

—MALCOLM X, THE AUTOBIOGRAPHY OF MALCOLM X

POT SPOTS: NEW YORK CITY

Long gone are the days of swinging Harlem jazz clubs where you'd score your weed, but there are other viable options. NYC is well known for the convenience of many delivery services. There's Fresh-Direct for groceries, Soap.com for other packaged goods, and a number of dealers who make house calls. The only tricky part is finding their phone numbers. Beware though, the weed there is pricey.

"Like brothers are smoking joints, getting the munchies, going out, trying to stick up Keebler elf houses. You see a bunch of brothers in the park harassing trees. 'Yo, I know you in there little elf, man. Just tell us which trees y'all make the cookies in.'"

—GREER BARNES

"Pulitzer Prize winning author Norman Mailer died last year at the age of eighty-four years old. For the last sixty years of this man's life, he drank to excess every day, he was married six times, he smoked pot, he stabbed his second wife. And I've never read one of his books, but I gotta tell you, I'm a huge fan."

—RON WHITE

"There would not have been a Cheech and Chong had there not been pot and Lenny Bruce. Just like there would not have been Motown, or the Beatles, or Bob Dylan, for that matter, because pot rules!"

—TOMMY CHONG, *CHEECH & CHONG: THE UNAUTHORIZED AUTOBIOGRAPHY*

"I AM FUCKING STONEY!"

—JOHN LENNON, *HERE, THERE AND EVERYWHERE: MY LIFE RECORDING THE MUSIC OF THE BEATLES*

"Judd Apatow is way better at being Kevin Smith now than Kevin Smith ever was. So Judd Apatow should do it for a while, and I should figure out something else, and weed has been fucking helpful with that."

—KEVIN SMITH

"I wondered, 'Would being stoned look way better on the film than acting stoned?'"

—EDWARD NORTON

"The detectives came in, and I hid behind this garbage. This garbage had so many roaches I was ready to give myself up. But then I took off my shirt, kicked in a door, walked right in past someone cookin', and I was like, 'Sorry about that.' This girl came out. She knew me. She was like, 'What you doing here with your shirt off?' I was like, 'Listen, can I talk to you for a minute?' I closed the door and I was like, 'How you doin'? Yo, five-O is right downstairs. Can I go through your front door?' She was a cool person."

—REDMAN

Neil Patrick Harris (as himself): What does the P.H. stand for in N.P.H.?

Harold (John Cho): Patrick Harris?

Neil Patrick Harris: No, common mistake. Poon Handler.

—*HAROLD AND KUMAR ESCAPE FROM GUANTANAMO BAY*

"I was at the point, you know, after you eat the drugs and you know you're going to be high, but you're not high yet, so you have to make all of your closing comments to everybody because you're not going to say another word for the rest of the night. So I'm giving my final thoughts, and Cyndi Lauper comes over, and she's like, 'Oh my God, I can't believe you're here. You should go on. I love your comedy. You should go on. . . . You should go on. You should go on!' . . . And then I don't know what happened after that."

—MARGARET CHO

HIGH CREDENTIALS: MARGARET CHO

She says she's given up pot— for now. The whole reason she stopped was because it didn't affect her anymore. Well, give it a little rest, and then come back, ready to be hit hardcore. In the meantime, she's still one of pot culture's favorite comedians, complete with a San Francisco upbringing, Bonnaroo appearances, and stories about her mom who doesn't get her. She may leave pot for a while, but she'll never leave us.

"I would like a nice, powerful, mind-altering substance. Preferably one that will make my unborn children grow gills."

"I just gave weed to a homeless man in front of paparazzi what was I thinking?"

"Now we take a look at the radar. Hey, the radar's pickin' up Mitch Miller! Sing along with Mitch, man! Baby . . . Gimme . . . your answer do, I'm half crazy, all . . . Where was I, man . . . ? Oh yeah, the radar's picking up a line of thundershowers. . . . However, the radar is also picking up a squadron of incoming Russian ICBMs, so I wouldn't sweat the thundershowers!"

"We'll be coming up with our own Cheech and Chong version of a game. The idea I'm working on now is 'Let's Make a Dope Deal' about dealers and growers."

"Rhys [Ifans] is great—he's one of those method actors and really lives the part. So he wanted to go on some real big benders with me to see how I am when I'm really off my head. . . . We went on a really heavy cocaine and weed session on one of his days off and I think it took its toll. But it'll probably look great in the film!"

"His 'long-range-plan,' he says, is to 'refine' these nerve-wracking methods, somehow, and eventually 'create an entirely new form of journalism.' . . . During one four-day period in Washington he destroyed two cars, cracked a wall in the Washington Hilton, purchased two French Horns at $1100 each and ran through a plate-glass door in a Turkish restaurant."

—EDITOR'S NOTE ABOUT HUNTER S. THOMPSON, *THE GREAT SHARK HUNT* (ON WHY THE BOOK WAS SOMEWHAT INCOMPLETE)

"In the old days, especially when I'd go to a concert—Johnny Winter, the Stones or Hendrix, I'd scream and get beat up and try to get on the stage. I got stomped by Grateful Dead guys for try'na get on the stage when they were on. And my foot got broken with the Stones."

—PATTI SMITH

AFTERWORD

I didn't smoke up once during the writing of this book. Who am I kidding? The actual number was much higher, and so was I.

Use these dope quotes for good and let these famous stoners inspire you. Tell nay-sayers to chill out or build that pumpkin bong that you've been dreaming of. Maybe you'll find a new movie to rent. (Classics are great too.) Or maybe you'll travel the world in search of prime grass. . . . Now, that would be awesome.

Hopefully you remember something from all this, man. Everything we do, we do for pot's sake, and this book is no different. We all smoke the good herb. It breaks it all down, evens the playing field. We come together as one. Marley would be proud.

And you'll never be alone. After all, you're not the only one who smokes—everyone lights up every once in a while. Just make sure you always pass the bong and share your brownies.

Before you go off on your merrily stoned way, I'll leave all of you fellow reefers out there with one final quote. From the loud and so very wise Wanda Sykes, in her book *Yeah, I Said It:*

"Man, as soon as I finish writing this book, I'm getting fucked up!"

Acknowledgments

The following websites were great resources for both their informative seed listings and/or their lists of and info on 420-friendly folks:

www.420magazine.com
www.cannabisculture.com
www.celebstoner.com
www.comedycentral.com
www.dailymotion.com
www.eonline.com
www.friendsofcannabis.com
www.google.com
www.grasscity.com
www.hightimes.com
www.imdb.com
www.kindgreenbuds.com
www.marijuana.com
www.marijuanareviews.com
www.marijuanatipster.com
www.strainreview.com
www.thefreshscent.com
www.weed-seeds.net
www.wikipedia.com
www.youtube.com

Further thanks to Arsenio, Eric, Stacey, Rob, Sara Collins, and the fine folks who kept me motivated via instant messaging.

DAILY BENDER

Want Some More?

Hit up our humor blog, The Daily Bender, to get your fill of all things funny—be it subversive, odd, offbeat, or just plain mean. The Bender editors are there to get you through the day and on your way to happy hour. Whether we're linking to the latest video that made us laugh or calling out (or bullshit on) whatever's happening, we've got what you need for a good laugh.

If you like our book, you'll love our blog. (And if you hated it, "man up" and tell us why.) Visit The Daily Bender for a shot of humor that'll serve you until the bartender can.

Sign up for our newsletter at
www.adamsmedia.com/blog/humor
and download our Top Ten Maxims No Man Should Live Without.